The Million LinkedIn Message

The story of how one single LinkedIn message opened the door to a £1,000,000 sale, and how you can start winning more business through LinkedIn messaging.

By Daniel Disney

www.danieldisney.net

First published in 2019 by Daniel Disney.

Copyright 2019 © Daniel Disney. All rights reserved.

ISBN: 9781086321562

Cover Designed by Daniel Disney

Doodles by Daniel Disney

Headshot photo by Shoot Me Now (David Green)

All rights reserved. Apart from any permitted use under UK copyright law, no part of this publication may be reproduced or transmitted in any form or by any means, electronic or mechanical, including photocopying, recording, or any information, storage or retrieval system, without permission in writing from the publisher or under licence from the Copyright Licensing Agency Limited. Further details of such licences (for reprographic reproduction) may be obtained from Copyright Licensing Agency Ltd, Saffron House, 6-10 Kirby Street, London, EC1N 8TS.

Any views expressed within this guide are the sole responsibility of the author and do not reflect the opinions of any other person, publisher, company or organisation.

This book is in no way authorized by, endorsed by, or affiliated with LinkedIn or its subsidiaries. All references to LinkedIn and other trademarked properties are used in accordance with the Fair Use Doctrine and are not meant to imply that this book is a LinkedIn product for advertising or other commercial purposes.

This book is intended to provide general information only. The author does not provide any legal or other professional advice. If you need professional advice, you seek advice from the appropriate licensed professional. This book does not provide complete information on the subject matter covered. This book is intended to be used only as a general guide.

What People Are Saying About This Book

No one spends more time on studying how to use LinkedIn to engage prospects. Off all the social sites, LinkedIn is the most useful, but only if you know how to use it. If you want to use LinkedIn, read and apply Daniel Disney's book.

Anthony Iannarino – Author of The Only Sales Guide You'll Ever Need, The Lost Art of Closing & Eat Their Lunch

Daniel is an authority in the Social Selling space and this book solidifies that notion even further. You will get actionable advice and more insight than you ever dreamed of when it comes to LinkedIn and the social game you need to be playing. Brilliant read! Pick this book up and start changing the game."

Dale Dupree – Leader of The Sales Rebellion

LinkedIn holds the golden keys to sales at all levels. Daniel Disney knows how to use the keys to open doors and close business. There are hundreds of LinkedIn "experts" but Daniel doesn't just talk the talk, he walks the walk. From creating The Daily Sales to closing The Million Pound Sale, Daniel's easy to follow tips will give you new ways to improve your LinkedIn results.

Alison Edgar – Author of Secrets of Successful Sales

LinkedIn is vital for your business, yet most people are not using it effectively. The UK's number 1 Social Selling expert, Daniel Disney, solves this problem by showing you easy-to-implement techniques and tips that will make your Linked profile shines and help you generate more awareness and revenue for your business. I've read many LinkedIn books, and this is my favourite. Don't delay and buy your copy now to make a difference in your business.

Niraj Kapur - Expert Sales Coach, Trainer and Author - Amazon bestseller Everybody Works in Sales

This book unlocks simple but powerful strategies for winning on LinkedIn. Whether you are a seasoned LinkedIn pro or a green, LinkedIn newbie, this book is for you. My favourites were the 25 message templates which are jam-packed with instructions for when and how to use them.

Daniel Disney is the real deal; he has real followers, real successes, and is the number one influencer on LinkedIn. That stands him out from the LinkedIn crowd as the go-to expert. If you're going to listen to one person on the subject of LinkedIn, make it him.

Better still, buy this book, read it on the plane/train/automobile (he has packed it with content, not waffle), and start applying it the moment you land.

Gavin Ingham - Founder of #IAM10 & Author of 'Be More, Do More, Sell More'

Daniel teaches me something every time I read his content on LinkedIn, and what I learned after his LinkedIn/Social Selling Masterclass has helped me generate some great results on social. After reading his new book, "The Million-Pound LinkedIn Message", I had no doubt straight away that this would be the reference guide for so many sellers out there.

You have given the roadmap for all to follow, the question you will pose to every reader is, what will they do with these golden nuggets? Will they make their own million-pound sale or watch while others make theirs?!

Steve Knapp – Founder of The Sales Growth Club, Expert Sales Coach, Trainer & Consultant

Although I had the good fortune to have worked directly for LinkedIn. Few people on or at LinkedIn impressed me with the frequency, consistency and relevancy of content to inspire salespeople to leverage social media as much as Daniel Disney.

His dedication to providing valuable content to the world's sales community is second to none. What I love about this book is that he gets deep, tactical and practical with excellent tips you can leverage to inspire greater confidence in your sales efforts on LinkedIn. Highly recommend reading and sending around your team.

James Ski, Former LinkedIn Director and now Founder & CEO of Sales Confidence - the world's largest B2B Sales community.

In a sea of wishy, washy blog posts and crappy video content from so called "social guru's"... Daniel has bucked the trend and put together a step by step guide to engineering success on LinkedIn that anyone can follow.

Will Barron – Host of The Salesman Podcast

It's rare that a book can connect with you as a friend, mentor you as a teacher, correct you as parent, and encourage you as a colleague. This book does exactly that. Daniel's informal voice and delivery make this book an easy read that you simply cannot put down. Even as I read it, I knew I'd be referencing the content, templates, and how-to tactics over and over again; it will be front-and-centre on my bookshelf.

Of particular note are the many templates that Daniel provides, along with the use-case instructions and explanations for each of them. Whether you're a novice or an industry veteran, you WILL get immediate value from them, and you WILL be using them over and over again. This book is a must-read and a must-share.

Darryl Praill – CMO at VanillaSoft & Host of The INSIDE, Inside Sales Podcast

Foreword by Chris Murray

Author of "The Extremely Successful Salesman's Club" and "Selling with Ease".

There are a couple of things I need to share with you about Daniel Disney before we start.

First of all - with regards to 'Social Selling' - he really knows what he's talking about. Secondly - with regards to life in general - he is one of the good guys.

And it's because of those two points, that - in this world of snake-oil salesmen and faux business gurus who are happy to take punters hard earned cash in exchange for advice that sounds great, but is almost certainly destined to fail – Daniel Disney stands out from the crowd and is definitely worth taking notice of.

The first time I met Daniel in person was at a large, national sales event. We were both due to deliver our keynote speeches on the same day and I was in the organiser's office checking over a couple of things, when this polite young man peered round the door and introduced himself.

Back then, The Daily Sales hadn't been around too long – but even so, he'd already managed to attract a following that numbered in the hundreds of thousands.

Now, I'd seen people pay huge amounts of money to cultivate lists like that before – so I asked him;

"That's an impressive audience, how much of it did you buy?"

To which, with a genuine look of shock, Daniel responded:

"Buy an audience? I don't think I'd know how to!"

That statement, made with the honest naivety of someone who wasn't aware of how many "thought leaders" cheat their way to popularity, told me everything I needed to know.

The man standing in front of me wasn't buying attention - completely the opposite - he was well on his way to mastering the art and science of Customer Attraction.

And when it comes to business development in the 21st century - customer attraction was the secret ingredient that only a successful few had worked out how to bake with.

What I didn't realise back then was that there was something else in the Daniel Disney recipe mix – he had started successfully combining Customer Attraction with effective Social Sales Interaction.

Customer Attraction together with Social Sales Interaction – and shortly afterwards, that combination just exploded.

Thing is, because it all came so easily and naturally to him, Daniel didn't seem to realise how rare or magical those particular pieces of business knowledge were – or why so many people found them difficult to implement.

To most people, it was like watching him pull a sword out of stone – which is a piece of cake if you're the one who can do it - but the deepest of mysteries if you can't.

Thankfully, in this book - The Million-Pound Linked Message - Daniel shares that knowledge with us.

This is an incredibly powerful and generous piece of writing – he takes us step-by-step through his system – and then shares dozens of templates and examples so that everyone who reads this can hit the ground running as soon as they've finished it.

You can dip in and out of this book if you need to, but there's so much you'll miss out on if you do.

My best advice;

Devour this book - page by page - and then go through it again and make notes. Focus on your current sales objectives and prospects and use the information Daniel shares here to design a complete sales strategy from start to finish. Then, when you have new sales challenges or a fresh set of prospective customers, come back and check it out again.

Because every time you familiarise yourself with the wealth of information in this book - and the multiple applications of its content – you will be building a knowledge bank and sales toolbox that will give you a genuine advantage over a large majority of your competition.

To your success,

Chris Murray - Author of The Extremely Successful Salesman's Club & Selling with EASE

This book is dedicated to four people:

Uncle Al – The man who inspired me to get into sales and taught me to be the best salesperson I could possibly be. Not a day goes by that I don't wish you were still here to guide me, to see what I've achieved and to see this book. I hope it would have made you proud.

Laurie – You've stood by me whilst I put everything I could into my career. When I worked late nights and weekends trying to grow The Daily Sales and my Social Selling Masterclass, you did everything you could to make it easy for me. I'm so lucky to have you in my life and will work as hard as I can to provide the best possible life for you and our boys.

Joshua and Lewis – My 2 sons, you are the reason I work so hard and are the ones who make it all worthwhile. I love you more than anything in this world and am so proud of you both, and the wonderful people that you are both growing up to be.

Thank you for being such a huge part of my world and being the driving force behind my work.

Chapters

CHAPTER 1: What's in This Book? – 11

CHAPTER 2: Introduction – 13

CHAPTER 3: My Background in Sales – 18

CHAPTER 4: The Prospecting Maze – 24

CHAPTER 5: Outbound Social Selling – 31

CHAPTER 6: No One Likes Spam – 38

CHAPTER 7: One Size Doesn't Fit All – 46

CHAPTER 8: The Million Pound LinkedIn Message – 49

CHAPTER 9: 25 LinkedIn Message Templates – 66

CHAPTER 10: What If They Don't Reply? – 118

CHAPTER 11: Pick Up the Phone! – 123

CHAPTER 12: Next Steps – 126

BONUS CHAPTERS

1 - Top Social Selling Tips – 128

2 - How to Build A Great LinkedIn Profile – 132

3 - Cold Calling Is Just Like Blockbuster – 139

4 - Social Selling in Just 15 Minutes Per Day – 143

5 - The ABC's Of Social Selling – 147

Firstly, thank you!

I want to start this off by saying a **HUGE** thank you for buying this book.

It means the world to me that you have bought a copy, it really does. I have taken the task of writing this book very seriously and have worked tirelessly to put together something that is as value packed and helpful as possible.

I would love to see you post a picture of the book on social media to see where in the world you are reading it. Anything you post about the book please do tag me in and I'll make sure I like and comment!

I really hope you enjoy reading it.

What's in This Book?

In this book, you will learn the true story of how one single LinkedIn message opened the door to what became a sale worth over £1,000,000.

You will learn about what Social Selling is, why it's important, and how to leverage social messaging to its full potential. I've packed in 25 tried, tested and proven message templates that can help you generate more clients and sales opportunities.

I've even added in some bonus Social Selling and LinkedIn tips to make sure you get as much from this book as possible! This includes a guide on building a strong LinkedIn profile and a step by step guide to generate results with Social Selling from just 15 minutes per day!

Who am I?

My name is Daniel Disney (no I'm not related to Walt Disney, that I know of any way!).

I'm one of the world's leading LinkedIn and Social Selling experts and am on a mission to help as many businesses, entrepreneurs, sales leaders and salespeople leverage it to its full potential.

Here are some of my achievements to date:

- **55,000+** LinkedIn Profile Followers
- **465,000+** LinkedIn Company Page Followers
- **£Millions** in Closed Revenue from LinkedIn
- **300+** Articles Published on LinkedIn
- **165 Million** Content Views In 2018
- **10,000+** New Followers Every Month
- **No.1** Most Influential Sales Expert on LinkedIn

Not only have I achieved a lot on LinkedIn, but I continue to do this every single day, even right now as I'm writing this book. I live and breathe Social Selling.

I now travel the world keynote speaking at events and training sales teams at companies large and small how to generate more clients and sales from LinkedIn and Social Selling.

You can find out more right here:

www.danieldisney.net

Introduction

Introduction

The world has changed…

The way we communicate to each other has been one of the biggest changes.

When I was younger, there was no such thing as mobile phones, no such thing as the internet, no email, no text and definitely no social media.

Over the last 25 years, A LOT has changed…

We now have so many different platforms to communicate with. We can pick up the phone and call someone; we can text someone, we can send an email to someone, we can send a video message, we can make a video call, we can also send social media messages to each other.

We're living in a very different world now, and as communication platforms have changed, a lot of the way things are done has changed.

Notably, the way we buy has changed. 25 years ago, if you wanted to book a holiday, you would phone up or visit a travel agent. Now, we follow travel pages on social media and book our holidays online without any human interaction.

With the B2B industry, the only way to reach prospects 25 years ago was to pick up the phone, send them a letter, send them a fax or head on over and visit their office. Fast forward to now, and you have all of the above AND email, social media, text, video and more. That's more than double the number of tools that salespeople need to learn, master and use.

Over recent years, social media has become a very BIG part of sales.

For a lot of people out there, including many decision-makers, social media is the first thing they check in the morning, the last thing they check at night, and it's what they check every 15 minutes throughout each and every day.

Now, as a salesperson this is a huge advantage! You have this tool that your prospects are using that you can leverage in so many ways. And this is where Social Selling was born.

Social Selling was first the phrase used to refer to the "Social" part of selling, the <u>relationship</u> part of selling. It is now, however, more commonly known and used for the use of social media in the sales process.

The rise of social selling was hit with some resistance, traditional sales experts and traditional sales teams didn't want to change, they didn't want to learn something new, so they kicked back.

Some social sellers then used this, and so the debate between cold calling and social selling was born.

The debate challenged whether social selling was here to replace cold calling, or whether it was just a simple phase, something that wouldn't last past a couple of years.

Were salespeople now making less calls and just sitting in front of LinkedIn doing nothing? Were over 50% of salespeople missing their sales targets because of LinkedIn?

Has LinkedIn become a huge distraction for salespeople, pulling them away from real revenue-generating activities?

Here's the reality, the real sales truth about modern day selling in 2019 and beyond, that you need to know:

Social Selling is as much sales as anything else. It can be used to find, create, grow and close sales opportunities.

It can also be used to close deals, manage relationships and gain referrals. It is a part of each stage of the process and one that more and more people are using each and every day.

With Social Selling, you can generate sales from your profiles, from social media searches, from personal brands, from content and engagement.

You can also generate opportunities from direct messaging on social media, and this is what this book is focused around.

My LinkedIn inbox is filled daily with TERRIBLE sales messages, as are the inboxes of many decision-makers out there. Messages that never get read, often get deleted and sometimes even get the sender blocked.

In this book, I'm going to show you how to write more effective messages, ones that actually generate results. Messages that get read and replied to, ones that open doors.

My Background in Sales

My Background in Sales

As far back as I can remember, I've been selling. As a young kid, around 7-8 years old, I noticed a lot of my neighbours were bored during the summer and so I set up a mini arcade in my garage and charged them to play the games. Every day my garage was packed.

Over that summer, I pocketed a nice sum of money and became hooked on the world of sales and business.

During school, I would go onto to launch and run a sweet selling business selling sweets and chocolates from my backpack. I'd get my mum to take me to the supermarket to buy stock, add a small premium and generate a nice profit.

I would then go onto launch a T-Shirt printing business as part of an entrepreneurial school scheme at 15 years old, which became hugely popular across the whole school and generated a very good profit.

After finishing school, I then set up an eBay business, which I went on to run successfully for over 10 years, buying and selling 2nd hand items. One of my biggest successes doing this included buying an old virtual pet toy (Digivice for those who remember) for 10p at a carboot sale and selling it for £100 on eBay. That's a pretty decent profit margin there!

At 16 years old, I got my first proper job, a part-time job on the checkouts at a local DIY store.

Within a month, the sales manager from the kitchens and bathrooms (big-ticket items) came and spoke to me. She said she had noticed me on the tills and working around the store and believed I could be very successful in the world of sales. She promoted me into the sales department, and my love of sales truly began.

Over the following years, I progressed from Sales Rep to Sales Supervisor, Sales Manager, Area Sales Manager, Regional Sales Manager, Head of Sales and Sales Director. For the last 8 years, I've worked in the B2B sector, predominately within the IT/Tech industry.

I've sold software, hardware, services and training, and it was during this time that LinkedIn really started to boom and become a much bigger part of the way we sell.

Now I need you to know something that's very important…

Whilst I am here writing a book called "The Million Pound LinkedIn Message", whilst I sit here now with a LinkedIn audience of over 500,000 followers, 300+ blogs written and £millions in revenue generated via Social Selling, there is one thing I really need you to know:

I used to HATE social media!

That's right, a social media "expert" who used to hate social media.

Here's the thing, I'm not someone who was born into using social media, I was around 18 years old when Facebook first launched and by that age, I felt no need to use it. Whilst I set up an account alongside my friends, I rarely used it. I was never someone who felt the need to document and share everything that I did.

I didn't want to use social media, and I didn't feel that I needed to. I had spent all of my life in a world without social media and was happy without it.

Two things changed though...

Firstly, social boomed. More social networks, more users and very quickly it became a big part of all of our lives.

I soon set up a Twitter account and Instagram account, but again, I didn't use them that often. I was only connected to close friends and family and sharing things with and for them.

What really changed for me, was when LinkedIn really came into the mix.

I'd been working in sales for nearly 10 years utilising traditional sales methods. I had knocked on thousands of doors; I had made thousands of cold calls, sent thousands of emails, presented in loads of meetings.

If there was a tool or method that would help me sell, I would use it and master it.

Now I can remember one day as I was making cold calls; an email came into my inbox. It was a "LinkedIn" connection request. I wasn't sure what it was, so I clicked through and saw that one of my customers had sent me a request.

Now on LinkedIn even if you don't have an account, people can send a request to your email address, encouraging you to then set one up.

I was hesitant at first, but I very quickly saw this social network that was very much like a huge online business networking group. A lot of my prospects and customers were using it, and it was full of information and opportunities.

I set up my account and started connecting with my existing customers and colleagues at my company. Following that, I started to connect with some of the prospects I was working on.

The more I used it, the more amazing opportunities I found within it, and before I knew it, I was generating more pipeline, creating stronger relationships, speeding up my sales cycle and closing more sales.

LinkedIn was like rocket fuel; it impacted and enhanced every part of the sales process.

Over the last 6 years, I have immersed myself in the world of LinkedIn and Social Selling, learning through trial and error and relentlessly looking to understand and master all aspects of it. I've read the books, watched the videos, listened to the podcasts but more importantly I've gone out and tried, tested and mastered it.

I came to work early to use it, worked through my lunch breaks, stayed after work until late and used it during my evenings in weekends.

It has been the driving force in me exceeding targets year on year, progressing quickly up the corporate ladder, building a business and going self-employed.

Whilst in this book I am going to show you how to leverage LinkedIn messaging to its full potential, rest assured it wasn't that long ago that like many of you reading this book, I had NO IDEA how to use LinkedIn!

What I will teach you in this book is what I have learned from writing and sending hundreds of different templates.

Nothing that I teach, and nothing in this book, is theory. It has all been tried and tested and proven to deliver great results.

So, sit back, get comfortable, have a pen ready, and let me show you how to REALLY use LinkedIn to sell successfully.

The Prospecting Maze

The Prospecting Maze

It wasn't that long ago that salespeople only had a few methods to contact prospects and customers.

They could pick up the phone and call them, send them a letter, send them a fax or see them face to face.

As time has gone on, technology has advanced, and we now live in a time where there have never been more platforms for communication.

Suddenly we have text, email, social media, video and more. As salespeople, our prospects are all using these different methods, and we now have more chances than ever to reach them. What an exciting time to be working in sales, right?!

Never before has a salesperson had SO MANY tools available to sell. Yes, it means we have more to learn and master, but it creates so many more opportunities to sell.

The side effect of having so many different platforms to communicate is that we each prefer and use different ones. Some people prefer the phone; some people prefer social media; some people prefer email.

There's no right or wrong here, just individual choice. You can complain that it's better to talk to a real person on the phone, but that won't change the fact that some people don't like doing it, including some of your prospects. The world changes, people change, the way we buy changes and so as salespeople, so must we.

So, here is how I see prospecting in 2019 and beyond:

I think one of the best ways to illustrate it is to use a finger maze puzzle...

You should have seen one of these maze puzzles before. Several doors go into the maze, but only one will lead to the end at the middle. You follow different paths with your finger or with a pen to try and get it right.

Now in our modern-day world, each of our prospects and customers sits in their own little maze. Even you, the reader, as a consumer and buyer, will sit in your own little maze.

Each door into the maze represents a method of communication. One door will represent the phone or cold calling; one door will represent email, one social media, one face to face, you get the idea. As we all know with these puzzles, only one (or two) doors will lead to the middle and in the modern-day prospecting maze, often only one or two doors will lead you to the prospect.

And this is what I call the modern-day prospecting maze!

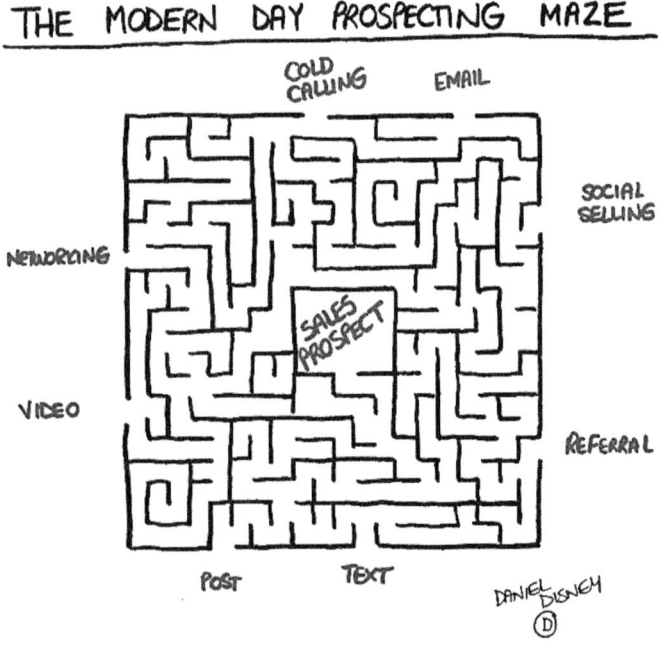

Now this is the important part...

EVERYONE IS DIFFERENT!

Each maze around each individual prospect will be different. For some prospects, the door that will get you to the prospect in the middle will be the phone. For some prospects, the door that will get you to the prospect in the middle will be emailed. For some, it will be social media.

And this is the very crucial reality for sellers today.

We have never had as many communication tools as we do today, and those will probably only continue to grow. 30 years ago, the prospecting maze consisted of far fewer doors, making it a lot simpler to reach prospects. It was also easier for prospects to ignore us.

There are many more doors now, which on the one hand makes it more complicated but on the other hand, means as a salesperson you've got MORE opportunities to reach prospects.

Let me give you an example...

Take me as a prospect, let's say you were trying to sell to me (which many people have done over the years and continue to do on a daily basis).

If you were to go through the cold calling door in my prospecting maze (in other words use cold calling to try and sell to me), you would end up at a dead end.

Personally, I don't answer cold calls, even though I've spent years making them and years training and leading salespeople making them, as a buyer, it's not a method that I personally respond to.

It doesn't matter how many times you try and call me; I won't answer.

I'm not alone with this; there are many people around the world, likely including many of YOUR prospects, who don't answer cold calls and will never answer cold calls.

The reason this point is so important is that there are still so many companies out there where their ONLY prospecting method is cold calling. There are also companies where cold calling is the core method alongside email.

If this is you, or your company, you're missing out on all of the prospects you could reach and sell to if you were to use other methods, such as LinkedIn and Social Selling.

Now as a salesperson, if you REALLY wanted to sell to me, let's say I was a huge prospect for you and one that you were so confident you could help, you would need to do something different.

Perhaps you'll connect with me via email, perhaps you'll see me at an event, but what will increase your chances is to connect and engage with me via LinkedIn.

And this is the reality of sales in 2019 and beyond. If you're restricting yourself to just one or 2 methods, you're simply limiting yourself. Some of your prospects will NEVER answer a cold call. Some will NEVER reply to your email. Some will ONLY talk to you if you engage with them well via LinkedIn or social media.

NOTE: I'm not saying one is better than the other; I want this message to be clear.

To reach the maximum number of prospects, you need to use ALL of the tools available. Some prospects will only ever talk to you via the phone. It's just important to appreciate now, however, that there is a percentage of your prospects that prefer digital communication.

In this book, I will show you one of the many ways you can leverage LinkedIn and social media to sell. LinkedIn messages are a hugely powerful tool when used right, trust me I've created and closed loads of B2B deals through LinkedIn messages.

The "Modern Day Prospecting Maze" is there to help you understand the prospecting landscape out there now.

The best sellers use as many of the doors available as possible to <u>increase</u> their chances of reaching the prospect in the middle.

Every time you're trying to sell to a prospect, put them in the middle of the prospecting maze and use it as a guide to help you approach each door. Check them as you go, attempt them multiple times and work hard to earn the attention of your prospect.

The prospecting maze doesn't just apply to prospecting either…

The maze applies to general communication as well. Just because you gain the opportunity through cold calling doesn't mean the phone is their platform of choice. Many customers that I won via a cold call actually end up being more responsive via email or social.

Use the maze as a guide for all parts of the process.

Outbound Social Selling

Outbound Social Selling

Over the last few years, I've noticed one thing…

A lot, and I mean A LOT of salespeople, sales leaders and even sales experts only think of social selling as an **INBOUND** generating activity. They see it as sharing content to generate inbound leads.

Whilst it is, of course, a very powerful inbound lead generating platform, it is equally a very powerful **OUTBOUND** lead generating platform.

For those who may not be familiar with these terms, inbound leads are leads that come into you. So, for example, someone visits your LinkedIn profile or reads content that you shared and then sends YOU a message enquiring to your product or service, that is seen as an inbound lead.

Inbound leads are more commonly generated by marketing departments, where they are then sometimes qualified and passed on to the sales department.

Outbound leads are more commonly generated by salespeople via prospecting activities where they go out and generate the opportunity. For example, cold calling will see salespeople phone up totally cold prospects and work to turn them into sales opportunities. They've have gone out and created an opportunity from nothing.

Right now, one of the biggest missed opportunities in sales is generating more outbound social selling opportunities.

Let me show you what I mean…

Say you're a B2B sales rep, and as part of a social selling push, you write an article on LinkedIn. That article goes out, gets some good engagement and then a nice little message pops up into your LinkedIn message inbox from a prospect saying they liked your blog and would like some more information or the opportunity to discuss the product or service you sell.

That would be an inbound lead.

I don't think many people out there would disagree with me here.

This is where the argument is often based that social selling is in fact not selling, but social marketing.

Based on that example alone, I would agree.

If you're creating content and then waiting for inbound leads to come in, that is simply a marketing activity.

Now let's say you wrote and published that article on LinkedIn. Perhaps you had a few inbound enquiries come through, which is great.

But let's say that you then decided to look at the engagement, the likes, comments and shares.

Whilst sifting through those engagements, you notice that someone who works within one of your prospect companies had actually clicked like on your blog.

If you then connect with them and send them a message to start a conversation, this is where <u>OUTBOUND</u> social selling comes in. This is where you are starting the conversation, not waiting for them to start it.

I'll share a real example of this with you:

A few years ago, whilst selling into the IT industry and trying to reach IT Managers/IT Directors, there was one company in particular that I was struggling to get through to.

They were a medium-sized business, around 200+ staff, and I could not get through to the decision-maker via cold calling or email. I had been trying to reach them for around 2 months.

One day I published an article on LinkedIn. It wasn't an article based on the IT industry, so wasn't aimed at my target prospects. Instead, it was an article on sales, the subject I knew I could write about a lot more effectively. When looking at the engagement, I noticed that a sales rep from within the company I was trying to prospect had clicked like on my blog.

TOP TIP

When you create and share content on LinkedIn, whether it's a blog, post, video, photo, etc., you can't see the people that "View" the content. You could get 1000 views, but you'll never be able to see who they are.

When they engage with the content, such as clicking "like", commenting or sharing the content, THAT'S when you can actually see them.

Once you can see them, you can then connect with them and use it to start a conversation with them. This is why I encourage everyone creating content on LinkedIn with the goal of generating sales and clients to drive as much engagement to their content as possible.

It's only through the engagement that you can actually see who is engaging and start talking to them.

After realising that this sales rep had clicked like, I knew I had an opportunity to find a different route to my target decision-maker. Not many content authors actually engage with their audience. If you click like or comment on a post and the author contacts you, that's pretty special!

I connected with the sales rep and sent them a nice simple conversational message (which you'll also find in the template chapter later on in this book):

> Hi John,
>
> *Thank you for clicking like on my article! I hope you enjoyed it; I'd love to know what your thoughts were on the subject?*
>
> Kind Regards,
> Dan

They replied straight away, and we started chatting. I didn't jump in trying to pitch them, neither did I jump in straight away asking for the phone number of their IT Director. Instead, I talked to them about the subject of the article which they liked. I asked them what it was they liked about it and what experience they had in that area. Just a nice few questions to get them to feel valued and open up.

We sent a few messages back and forth, building a nice little bit of rapport, where I had then earned the opportunity to discuss what I was selling.

I then mentioned that I had been actually trying to reach their IT Director to discuss what I was selling. They were more than happy to make an introduction and actually went on to arrange a phone call for me with them.

After that phone call, I was then able to progress it into a meeting and eventually go on to win that sale.

I would argue very strongly that is outbound selling.

It's no different to cold calling someone; you are sending someone a message who doesn't necessarily know you, with the aim of creating a sales opportunity.

Just like a cold call, some won't reply/answer, and some will. The ones who do reply you then work on to turn into real sales opportunities.

It's time to start using social selling for both inbound AND outbound selling!

Most salespeople, in my experience, are either sending terrible sales pitch messages OR just not using social in any way to generate outbound opportunities.

LinkedIn messaging is one of the most powerful ways you can leverage Social Selling. It is absolutely no different, in my opinion, to cold calling.

In many ways, it can be a much warmer version, with the opportunity for you to have already connected with them, built credibility, trust and started building rapport.

This can help build a much stronger foundation to your buyer/seller relationship, one that can build a much stronger and longer lasting relationship on.

InMail VERSUS Message

For those of you who aren't sure what the difference between a LinkedIn InMail and a LinkedIn message, let me clarify for you.

A LinkedIn message is a message you send to a direct connection on LinkedIn. Someone who you have connected with, they have accepted, and they are now a 1st degree connection.

NOTE – If you are only "**Following**" them on LinkedIn, whilst you will be able to see their activity, you will not be able to message them directly. This is only possible when you are connected with someone.

A LinkedIn InMail is a message sent to someone that you are NOT connected with. You can only send these with LinkedIn Premium or LinkedIn Sales Navigator, and they come with a limited amount each month.

The templates in this book are designed for LinkedIn messages, to send to people that you are directly connected with. That being said, a lot of these would work on InMail as well.

What I will say is that you will often achieve a greater response sending them to connections, as a normal message compared to an InMail to people who have no idea who you are.

No one likes Spam

No one likes Spam

THIS IS VERY IMPORTANT! PLEASE READ!

In this book, I'm going to show you how one single LinkedIn message opened the door to a sale worth over £1,000,000.

What I need you to know and remember is that this was a 100% personal and individual message, not a spam one sent out to hundreds or thousands of prospects.

This message template, and the others included in this book will work best if you send them to qualified prospects on an individual basis.

Spam selling really isn't a strong strategy in sales anymore, copy and pasting generic messages and sending them to all of your connections on LinkedIn will struggle to yield a positive response. What does work is sending personalised messages to relevant people.

NO ONE LIKES SPAM!

I'm sure you don't like receiving spam messages, I bet even the people SENDING the spam messages don't like receiving them!

Yet I would bet that around 80-90% of the LinkedIn messages sent right now are considered spammy messages.

(Spammy messages are sales messages sent to prospects who don't need or want your product or service, often in an aggressive or sleazy sales style).

Please, when reading this book and using these templates, make sure you understand I only ever approach prospects with these message templates that I have qualified myself and am confident I can help.

Not only will you save time from sending hundreds of wasted messages, but you'll also increase your chances of conversion and success.

Unfortunately, when you don't do this, you'll end up sending messages to the wrong people. Perhaps they'll ignore it, perhaps the won't. Maybe they'll show their friends, or worse, maybe they'll post it on LinkedIn for all of their network (and anyone's network who engages with it).

Let me share with you some of the messages that I get on a regular basis in my LinkedIn inbox!

EXAMPLES

My inbox is filled with LinkedIn messages daily, and unfortunately, 80% of them are terrible (one of the biggest motivations behind me writing this book).

Not only are 80% terrible, they are also not relevant to me. The sales rep sending them could have seen this had they just spent 1 minute looking at my profile.

I'm going to share a few of them with you; I won't share who they are from, that wouldn't be fair!

But if you read these and know deep down you know that you've sent ones like this; hopefully this will be an eye-opener...

The WAY TOO LONG Message

Hi Daniel,

I trust this email finds you well. Thank you for your interest in the apprenticeship programme, I've attached some files for more information.

With the Government's introduction of new Funding Rules and no age restrictions, there has never been a better opportunity for businesses to upskill existing staff or future proof the business with an apprentice coming in at an entry or junior level position.

a registered provider of the Governments Skills Funding

With training centres in London and over 4 years' experience, led the way in providing specialist training from SME's through to some of the best known corporate companies in the UK.

THE "COPY + PASTE" EMAIL MESSAGE

New Government Funding Rules:

Under 50 Staff
Apprentice or Staff Aged 16-18 - Fully Government Funded
Apprentice or Staff Aged 19+
90% Government Funded – 10% Employer Contribution

50 Plus Staff Apprentice or Staff Any Age - 90% Government Funded – 10% Employer Contribution

Our Curent Programme Focus

- Level 3 Digital Marketer

As you will note from the attached our training programmes start at level 3 and have the option to progress further.

Please let me know when it would be a good time to speak with you.

Kind Regards,

I have had to cut this up into 3 sections to be able to fit into one single slide; it was WAY too long! You can tell it's been copied and pasted from an email, which is not a strategy I would recommend at all.

LinkedIn messaging is more of an instant messaging platform over an email platform. It's designed for short conversational messages.

You'll see as you read through this book that these light, conversation-starting messages work so much better than copy and pasted emails like this.

Keep them short, keep them valuable and keep them conversational.

However, they can get a little too short sometimes…

So, whilst this example was of a message that was way too long, here are a couple of examples of messages that I've received that are way too short:

The WAY TOO SHORT Messages

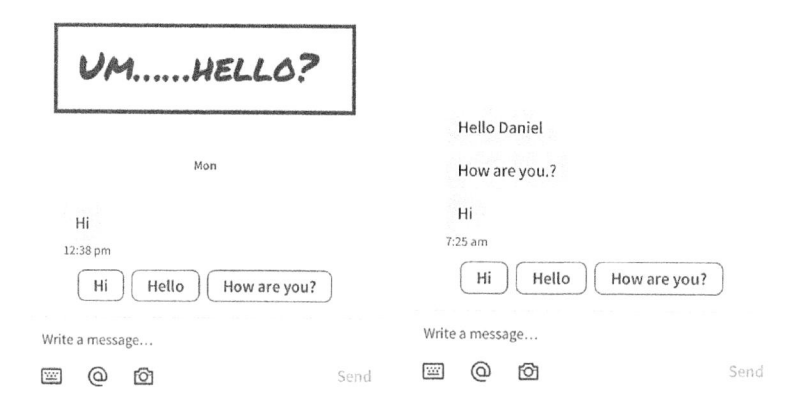

Um......hello?

```
                    Mon                          Hello Daniel
                                                 How are you.?
   Hi                                            Hi
   12:38 pm                                      7:25 am
   [ Hi ] [ Hello ] [ How are you? ]             [ Hi ] [ Hello ] [ How are you? ]
   Write a message...                            Write a message...
   ⌨  @  ⌖              Send                     ⌨  @  ⌖              Send
```

I also get messages that quite simply just say "Hi"!

Again, not a strategy I would ever recommend if you actually want to generate results from LinkedIn and Social Selling. In fact, I don't think I even send my friends messages like this, let along prospects or customers.

Both of those messages above were from people I have never spoken to before, nor did I know them either. This was the first time they had ever spoken to me, and they decided to go with just "Hi".

Whilst LinkedIn messaging is a more instant-message conversational style platform; this is perhaps a little too extreme. You want to find that sweet spot in between where it is light and conversational, but still professional. It needs to capture their attention and encourage them to want to reply.

There are a few other examples of messages that are perhaps a little too chatty or a little too needy…

FEB 22

TOO CHATTY....

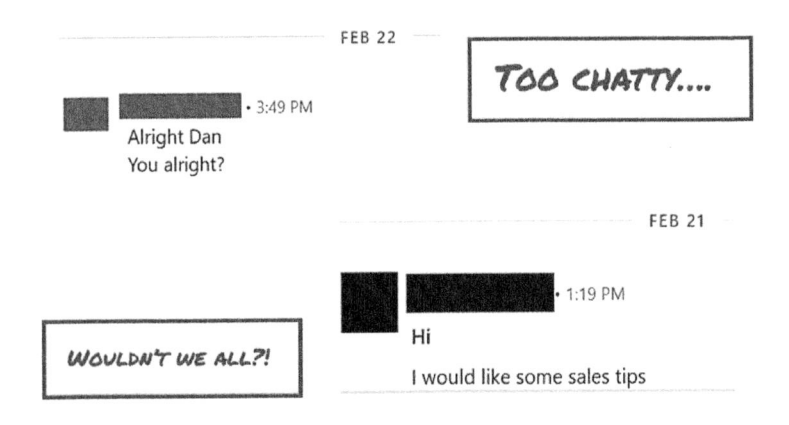

• 3:49 PM
Alright Dan
You alright?

FEB 21

• 1:19 PM
Hi
I would like some sales tips

WOULDN'T WE ALL?!

I mean some of my friends might message me saying "you alright", but not a complete stranger who I have never spoken to before and who would later go on to try and pitch me their product.

This is why I was so motivated to write this book. My inbox (like many others out there) is filled DAILY with messages like these or very sales driven messages.

Unfortunately, the majority of sales-driven messages are selling a product that I have no need for at all. Worst yet, the salesperson sending them could have found that out had they spent just 1 minute looking at my LinkedIn profile.

There is one more bad message style that is one of the worst out there right now...

I believe it's a style that has unfortunately been taught by some of the other LinkedIn/Social Selling experts out there, but it is one that is hated by decision-makers and one that I find quite shocking myself.

I see so many posts from decision makers about it...

It gives the impression that you value YOUR time above theirs, which isn't something I personally would recommend.

The "Here's MY Calendar Link" Message

> ○ Mobile • 40m ago
>
> across all the major job boards?
>
> We have accounts with the leading sites, TotalJobs, Jobsite, Monster, Reed, CV Library, Indeed, etc, and can help you advertise across them all for cheap and gain access to their CV databases.
>
> Let me show you how it works with a quick demo:
> https://calendly.com
>
> Kind regards

> ARE YOU MORE IMPORTANT THAN YOUR PROSPECT?

This is the "here is **MY** calendar link for **YOU** to book a meeting with me" message. It's one of the most ego-driven examples of selling I've seen in modern-day sales.

It's very much like the cheesy, sleazy salespeople of the past. The type that would walk up to you and make you feel like it was you who needed them. This isn't the way sales is anymore!

It suggests that your time is more valuable and important than the time of your prospects, which isn't a great way to present yourself when trying to win business.

Don't get me wrong; online calendars are great! They're super-efficient and effective and making booking meetings with prospects and customers. When your constantly going back and forth trying to find a good date, they really help.

However, using them in this way isn't something I would personally recommend.

As a salesperson, you need to <u>EARN</u> the right to a conversation, demo or meeting.

After you've given value, built a relationship and qualified them as a prospect, then is the time that you can ask THEM if they would be happy to arrange a phone call or face to face meeting.

If they are happy, then you can send them a link to your calendar. Even then though I would still recommend asking them what dates/times work best for them. The sheer act of sending them your calendar link places value in your own time above them.

Only if you've gone back and forth a few times and are struggling to find a date that works for both of you, only then does the online calendar link truly provide value in sales.

The only other opportunity that I would say does justify the use of online calendar links is if they approach you earlier on and ask for some dates. That is also an opportunity where sending a link to your online calendar can provide value.

Respect your prospects time, respect their position in the process and their value to you and treat them well. Use messages to give value, open conversations and start strong relationships with your customers.

One Size Doesn't Fit All

One Size Doesn't Fit All

Before we dig into the million-pound message, I need you to understand that one size doesn't fit all.

This is the same for cold calls, the same for sales emails, the same for face to face meetings. If you take one approach and apply it to every prospect you try and sell to, you'll rarely succeed.

Everyone is different!

Each of your prospects is an individual, different in their own unique ways. One of the most important skills a salesperson can possess is the ability to adapt and mirror their prospects and customers. This is the same rule with Social Selling; it's important to treat each prospect as an individual.

Sales work best when you stop trying to sell to anyone and everyone and start selling to the people who actually need what you sell. It's not about throwing as much stuff onto the wall and seeing what sticks, it's about being smart, genuine and authentic.

Whilst the core message in this book may have unlocked a huge sale for me, it doesn't mean you can copy it, paste it and send it to every single one of your prospects and the sales will start flooding in!

Different prospects, different products and different industries will all play a role in the type of messaging you should use on LinkedIn.

Therefore, I didn't just want to share the million-pound message with you; I wanted to provide you with as many proven LinkedIn message templates as possible.

After I take you through the story of the million-pound LinkedIn message I'm going to share with you 25 tried, tested and proven LinkedIn messages.

Each template will have notes that will hopefully help you determine which of your prospects would benefit from it and how best to use it.

I'd then highly recommend finding the templates that suit each individual prospect. It may be challenging at first, but like with anything once you learn it and practice it, it will soon become routine.

It's changing your mindset from only trying to sell products, and instead working with people to help solve their problems.

The Million Pound LinkedIn Message

The Million Pound LinkedIn Message

Let's dig into the core part of this book.

I'm going to tell you the whole story now of how one individual LinkedIn message opened the door to one of the biggest sales in my career.

I will go into as much detail as I can as the process done before and after the message are equally as important as the message itself.

Here we go…

Setting the scene

Whilst working for a large IT company in the UK, my team sold IT training packages mainly to SME's (small to medium-sized employers).

When selling to SME's, it's often very easy to reach decision-makers via cold calling, well it certainly used to be back then, as there aren't as many people or layers in the business.

We would go in and present a variety of training packages valued between £3,000 and £18,000. The sales process often took around 1-2 months from prospecting through to closing.

Most of the time we would cold-call first to find the decision-maker and aim to either email information over or book a meeting straight of the call.

During the meeting, we would then run through needs, listen and learn about the prospect. After that, we would go back, put together a proposal and call them or meet them again to run through it.

It was a highly competitive market; we had a lot of competitors, some bigger than us, some cheaper than us. A lot of our success came down to us either being the first to contact the prospect or our ability to build stronger relationships.

Following some really rapid growth, and as the top-performing person in sales, I was tasked with bringing on new large corporate clients to our portfolio. I very quickly found that cold calling was not as effective as it was with smaller companies!

Complex organisational structures and good gatekeepers made it very hard to get in front of the decision-maker. I learned how to do it effectively, but there were some companies that were extremely challenging.

I was working on a few very big companies, global companies with multi £Billion+ turnover. After once again getting stuck at the gatekeeper on a cold call, I decided to look for other ways in.

One thing popped into my head; I wonder if the decision-maker is on LinkedIn?

I didn't have a name of who the decision-maker was, only a few job titles that I was currently working with. I was looking for HR Managers, L&D Managers and IT Managers (and above).

After a quick search, there they were! I popped onto their profile, had a read and soon qualified that this was the person I needed and wanted to speak to.

The first step is to connect with your prospect.

LinkedIn InMail's are ok, but they're no different (in some ways worse) than a cold call. When you connect with someone you are able to send them a LinkedIn message directly, which is far more effective, compared to an InMail which is sent to someone you aren't connected with.

Similar to most of the messages I get, most of the InMail's are even MORE salesy. They're colder and often never personalised, just more copy and paste jobs.

To be able to send a direct message, you need to connect with them first.

Let me just pause this story for a minute whilst I talk you through this stage:

When you go on their profile, if they're a 2nd degree connection, you'll see the option to "**Connect**". It's a nice blue button just under their LinkedIn banner.

NOTE: If they're a 3rd degree connection, you won't see the "**Connect**" button, but instead will see a "**Message**" button with a little lock image next to it. This means you can only message them via InMail's if you have LinkedIn Premium or LinkedIn Sales Navigator.

In the past, there would be no way that you could send this person a connection request; however, LinkedIn have changed that now.

If you click the "**More...**" button next to the "**Message**" button, it will open up a section with 4 options: Share Profile, Save to PDF, Connect and Report/Block.

If you click the "**Connect**" option, it will be the same as clicking the connect button with a 2nd degree connection.

When you click on the "**Connect**" button, it will prompt a little pop up that will say:

"You can customize this invitation

LinkedIn members are more likely to accept invitations that include a personal note.

Add note   –   Send now"

Would you like to customise this request? YES! It can be very helpful, depending on the prospect, to personalise your connection request.

However, personalising can work against you! Not only are there a huge amount of people out there that will be more than happy to connect to you without a personalised request, sometimes personalising it can discourage people from connecting.

I get tonnes of requests daily, and a large percentage of the personalised ones are personalised with a sales pitch! This does not help increase your chances of getting it accepted, it often has the complete opposite effect.

From my own experience connecting and messaging hundreds of decision-makers, the higher up the or more senior the prospect, the more beneficial personalising will be.

The key is to NOT personalise it with a sales message. There are several templates you can use for this, most of the time I go with something simple like:

> *"Hi Sally,*
>
> *I'd love to connect,*
>
> *Kind Regards,*
>
> *Dan"*

Simple, personal and in no way present me as someone who is going to try and sell to them. This isn't a sure-fire guaranteed way to get them to accept; some people need more than this.

Some will need you to engage with their content a bit first. I judge it by how active THEY are on LinkedIn. If they are quite active and have a large network (over 1,000), then that tells me they are going to quite likely to accept my request.

If they're not very active and have a smaller network, then it's more likely that I'll need to build some rapport first.

Back to the story...

In this case, they were active, so I went with the small, simple personalisation. Within 30 minutes they had accepted my request, a great start to the process!

Sometimes, it can be smarter after connecting to engage with their content a bit first or share your own content for them to see. You can do this over a few days, or 1-2 weeks+ to build some foundations before you go in to start a conversation. Again, make a judgement on the prospect and also the proposition you are offering.

In this case, I was very confident that this company would need and want the product I was selling (from qualification I had already done). The prospect was active on LinkedIn, which showed me that sending a message straight away could work well.

What I have found from experience is that the higher up the chain that you're pitching, the more direct you should be. If you're selling to Directors or C-Level positions, then it can often work better to just go straight in with a message.

BUT

Obviously, it needs to be a well-crafted message...

And this is where the £1,000,000 LinkedIn message was born.

Remember this is NOT a sales pitch

This is not about you listing loads of features and benefits or telling them how amazing your product and company are.

It's not about you trying to jump in bed with them straight away.

It is NOT some spammy message.

It is NOT a copy and paste job.

It is a simple message with one simple goal...

To start a conversation with a potential customer.

Here it is...

> *"Hi Sally,*
>
> *Thank you for connecting! I work for a company called X who is one of the UK's leading providers of IT Training. I would love to learn a bit more about what you're currently using for that?*
>
> *Kind Regards,*
> *Dan"*

It was that simple.

Before you start to feel underwhelmed by this message, this is the message that opened the door to a sale valued over £1,000,000. It was this single simple message that did that. Not a cold call, not an email, not a letter, not a text, not a video, not the type of LinkedIn messages I get in my inbox, but this simple message.

That particular decision maker wouldn't take cold calls, had an email inbox filled daily with spam, yet loved spending time on LinkedIn.

In sales, we know simple works best. It's when we overcomplicate things that they often go wrong.

This was a small conversational prospecting message that thanks them for connecting, explains who we are and what we do and asks them a question about what they may already have in place for that product or service.

As a decision-maker reading this, I'm not overwhelmed by some sort of huge message or something that comes across in an aggressive way.

It makes me think of that particular product or service and whether or not I'm happy with what I've currently got, whether I need it or whether I may want to change it.

Of course, this doesn't work for everyone.

As I mentioned earlier, this isn't something you can just copy and paste a thousand times. However, with the right prospect, this can and does work.

For me, on this occasion and for this particular prospect, I got a reply back within an hour.

I can actually remember the exact moment; I was having lunch with a colleague (fish and chips with a cold can of lemonade) and decided to check my phone. Logging into

LinkedIn, I saw the little notification on the messages, opened it up and was met with a reply.

Let's just say I did a little fist pump in the air when I read the reply and saw there was potential opportunity brewing right there!

This was the reply I received:

> *"Hi Dan,*
>
> *Thank you for your message. This was well-timed as it is something that we've not done before but are actually starting to look at options now. Could you send me some more information about what you offer, please?*
>
> *Kind Regards,*
> *Sally"*

It was a fantastic response; it showed interest and a potential opportunity.

This is another very important part of the process, what do you do next?

Some salespeople will try and send a load of information into another LinkedIn message, which I must advise against! LinkedIn messages are designed to be light and conversational; the moment more detail and information comes into it, it's time to move the conversation away from LinkedIn.

Only on specific situations will the conversation stay on social, depending on the prospect and the complexity of what it is you're selling.

The information I needed to send was best sent via email, something which I still do to this day. My goal next is to try and get an email address with permission to send them information.

I replied:

> *"Hi Sally,*
>
> *That's great to hear, what was the best email address to send the information across to?*
>
> *Kind Regards,*
> *Dan"*

An email address soon followed, and I was then able to get to work on crafting an effective sales email that contained some more information but was designed to continue the conversation and ideally move it onto a phone call or face to face meeting. Nothing too long, just to the point, engaging and packed with the right information.

The email described our packages in more detail, explained some of the other companies we had worked with and the results (ROI) that they had achieved. The email ended with: "If it's something that you're interested in I would love to pop in and explore in a bit more detail".

A meeting was confirmed, where I learned all about the company, their past, present and plans for the future. It was clear they had a real need for what I was selling; however, I was also made aware they were exploring other companies as well.

We explored how this product could fit well, how it could work, and what the process would be following this meeting. They had to run it past the CEO, before looking at a more detailed plan of action.

A couple of weeks later I followed up with a phone call, the meeting had been delayed with the CEO, but they were pushing for it this week.

I then received a phone call later this week after that meeting had happened informing me, they were keen to move forward and wanted me to come in to work out a more detailed plan of implementation and next steps.

There were 2 more meetings and several emails back and forth while the final proposal was drawn up and then finally presented. I spent hours building the perfect proposal, making sure it answered their questions and helped them.

The process from start to finish took around 5 months. After finally presenting the proposal, I was met with the response I had worked so hard for:

80 units at £15,000 each, across 4 years was ordered, a deal worth a total of £1,200,000.

One of the biggest sales of my entire sales career.

That whole deal, that whole million-pound deal, started with one single LinkedIn message.

Not a cold call, not a cold email, not a referral, not a networking event, but one simple single LinkedIn message.

It's not the phone VERSUS social selling…

One of the biggest debates that has raged across sales for several years now is the whole phone/cold calling versus social selling.

It gets heated, emotional and often quite aggressive. Unfortunately, I've been involved in several debates over recent years, but my message has always been this:

It's not the phone/cold calling VERSUS social selling; it's the phone/cold calling <u>ALONGSIDE</u> social selling.

As you'll see from this example of the million-pound LinkedIn message, it was social selling that created the

Opportunity and the phone that then progressed it, alongside email and face to face.

It was the combination of all of these platforms that allowed me to sell effectively and win this deal. I guarantee there would have been other salespeople approaching this prospect but only using the phone or even only using social.

As Tony J Hughes describes it perfectly in his book, COMBO Prospecting, it's only by using all of these tools together that you can strategically sell to the modern-day customer.

The £1,000,000 wasn't won JUST on social but was won through a combination of all the key tools out there. It was, however, created on social, and this is why I'm so passionate about Social Selling. Had I not utilised social selling, I may never had created or won this deal.

WHY WOULD YOU ONLY FISH IN JUST ONE....?

Fishing for Customers

LinkedIn · Phone · Email

YOU CAN FISH IN ALL!

The Process

Here's a summary of that process:

Stage 1 - Find decision-maker on LinkedIn

Stage 2 - Send personalised connection request

Stage 3 - Send prospective message.

Stage 4 - Ask for email to send information.

Stage 5 - Send email with information

Stage 6 - Follow up and arrange phone call to discuss

Stage 7 - Have phone call and follow up with email

Stage 8 - Arrange face to face meeting

Stage 9 - Have face to face meeting

Stage 10 - Send follow up email

Stage 11 - Build Proposal

Stage 12 - Present Proposal

Stage 13 - Follow up to close deal

Stage 14 - Close deal and sign paperwork

Stage 15 - Implement product/service

Stage 16 - Gain referrals and a recommendation

And there you have it...

One simple LinkedIn message aimed at starting a prospecting conversation, that turned into an email with more information, which turned into a phone call to discuss in more detail, which turned into a face to face meetings to discuss a potential opportunity which after a few more emails and meetings turned into a signed deal.

As I've already mentioned, that message template won't work for everyone.

This is why I've included 25 templates in this book!

What I hope you'll see is that the £1,000,000 message and all of the other templates have a few things in common...

They're light, conversational and serve the same purpose of STARTING the conversation. In my experience, this is the best way to leverage LinkedIn to sell.

Right now, in 2019, a percentage of decision-makers still prefer the phone as a communication method. However, younger decision-makers are rising, and current decision-makers are becoming more digital-savvy.

There are more and more people buying products, both B2C and B2B, through total digital conversation.

I currently have several key B2B clients where the whole conversation, from prospecting, qualifying, presenting and closing, is done entirely on LinkedIn or other social media platforms.

DON'T BE A SALES DINOSAUR!

EMBRACE CHANGE
EMBRACE SOCIAL
EMBRACE DIGITAL

Digital customers need digital sellers, and so now is the best time to start learning and mastering the digital and social selling landscape. Learn to master all the aspects, including social media messaging.

Don't be a sales dinosaur...

Don't complain that people should talk on the phone.

Don't complain that people are scared to make calls.

Accept this is the way of the world and if you want to succeed you need to embrace it.

Embrace the change, adapt to the new sales landscape and evolve to continue thriving in your sales career.

Learn these message templates, find the prospects they are best suited to, personalise them and feel free to make changes. You should know your prospects better than anyone, use these as guidance to help craft the ultimate message for your prospects.

25 LinkedIn Message Templates

25 LinkedIn Message Templates

There are so many ways you can craft effective LinkedIn messages, with the key always being to personalise it to each individual prospect and customer.

I'm going to share with you a set of templates that I have used over the years to generate sales opportunities selling IT, Software, Advertising, Training, Events and Consultancy.

NOTE - INSERT NAME – You will notice that each template starts with this. It is because this is so important.

Personalisation is crucial when it comes to effective sales messaging. As I mentioned earlier on in the book, messaging becomes significantly less effective when you adapt the "copy and paste" approach. It is worth the effort in ensuring that you use their name to help deliver the optimal impact of the message.

The Goal of the Message

You will notice that most of these templates focus on the goal of opening the conversation or gaining an email address to send information across. When it comes to social selling and LinkedIn, this approach has become the most successful in my experience, compared to outright asking for a phone call or face to face meeting.

By offering to send more information with the aim of securing an email address, you open the doors to conversation. Going in for the kill and asking for a call or meeting is extremely "salesy" and aggressive.

"But Dan, that's what we do when we cold call, we want to speak to them and get a meeting".

True, but that's why ROI on cold calling is often below 2-3%. The phone and social are different platforms; we use them both very differently.

I fully suggest you leverage cold calling and make your 50-100+ calls per day or whatever you need to make. However, when leveraging social selling and more specifically LinkedIn messaging, my advice is to use it to start conversations or get your foot in the door where you can then EARN the opportunity to arrange a phone call or meeting.

You'll notice the user of SOFTER words as well...

Throughout these templates, you'll notice words like "Believe", "Possibly", "Potentially", "Maybe" etc. These are soft words and ones that aren't often encouraged in sales; however, when it comes to Social Selling and utilising messaging on LinkedIn, it's these words that I've found deliver the best results.

Instead of "Hi my name's Dan, and I'm confident I could help you with my product", writing it like this "Hi my name's Dan, and I believe we may be able to help with you this product."

You avoid coming across as ego-driven or arrogant and also avoid sounding like an aggressive salesperson. Instead the message and tone are focused far more on helping them and how you believe you may be able to.

I've tried and tested stronger, more assertive language in LinkedIn messages, and I've tried and tested softer language, and, in my experience, the softer language delivers a far greater response rate.

We have more confident and information savvy prospects and customers now compared to before, and they require a much more value giving than value taking approach. Don't force your way in with them, earn it.

Let's get into these templates...

These templates are designed to be used as guides, please do make custom changes to ensure they are fully personalised to your prospect and their individual situation. Feel free to move them around a bit in their format, if you feel it suits your prospect, their position or industry better. These are here to help you start and provide a basic structure.

Now there are loads of variations of templates like this, including lots of other styles that are used. What I've done over the years is test as many templates as possible to find the ones that generate the best possible results.

After testing hundreds of templates over the last 6 years through my own prospecting, with my sales teams and with the businesses I have trained, here are the 25 that have proven to be the most effective:

1. <u>The Introduction Message</u>

> "Hi (Insert Name)
>
> Thank you for connecting. I work for a company called (Insert company name) who are one of the world's/regions/local areas of (insert product/service). If I can ever help you, please do let me know,
>
> Kind Regards,
>
> Dan"

This works really well as a friendly initial introduction. You're not asking for anything, just letting them know what it is you do and that you are there if they need it.

If you catch someone at the right time where they need what you sell, this will generate a good response and is a great way to start the conversation because you haven't been aggressive or pushy, just a nice introduction.

Some salespeople use this template, but instead of ending it with "if I can ever help", they go straight in and ask for a phone call or meeting.

This often comes across as pushy and given the high chance you've never met nor spoken to this person before, doesn't give them much reason to speak to you. Instead, keep it open, let them know what you do and then step away to focus on other social selling activities such as personal brand and content.

I'd advise sending this message and then start working on engaging with their content. Like some of their posts, comment on some of their posts, get your name seen by them and show interest, knowledge and value.

BONUS TIP – Writing comments is a great way of getting your name and picture seen by your prospect and also a great way of showing your knowledge, experience and interest in your industry. Comments add the value of actually showing your name, where as a "like" will only show a small picture of your face.

Take it a step further by sharing your <u>own</u> content on a regular basis. This will build your personal brand and build trust within them.

Then after a few weeks, pop them another message more focused on a potential ROI and asking to send them some more information (you'll see some examples of these messages below). What you will have achieved is hopefully putting yourself on their radar.

They'll start getting used to seeing your name in a positive way through the content you share. They'll recognize you and you'll become someone of value, and not just another salesperson who is ONLY trying to sell them something.

This will warm them up and build a far greater foundation for the relationship, where you are on a much more level playing field and not chasing them.

2. The ROI Introduction

> Hi (Insert Name),
>
> I wanted to pop you a quick message to let you know that we help businesses (insert ROI) with (insert product).
>
> If you ever need (insert product) please feel free to get in touch for an informal chat,
>
> Kind Regards,
> Dan

A slight adjustment to the first template, this one is another introduction style post but with the addition of ROI (Return on Investment), or in other words what will they get in return for buying your product.

I've used this when approaching more senior decision-makers and C-Level prospects as the ROI that you include cuts through the noise more effectively. It will stand out compared to the typical sales message by getting straight to the point, not dancing around with old fashion sales tactics that are just too obvious now.

Showing them what you could do for them can act like a strong bait though. I used this one with a recruitment company recently that bought me in to help them reach their prospects more effectively; we crafted a message following this particular template which proved really effective:

> *Hi (Insert Name),*
>
> *I wanted to pop you a quick message to let you know that we help businesses save up to 80% of their recruitment costs with our straight to job board system.*
>
> *If you would ever like to know a bit more, please do let me know,*
>
> *Kind Regards,*
>
> *Joe Bloggs.*

Again, this is a nice soft introduction style message, but one that is attached with a potential ROI, which then becomes bait. The ROI stands out and as a decision maker reading this it makes think about the impact that ROI could have on them.

As a salesperson, by sending this message out to prospects, it's like casting fishing rods out into the river or sea. If there are fish (prospects) who are ready to bite, they'll bite and reply, and you can then reel them in.

If they are not ready, then that message will sit out there until they are (whilst you utilise other social selling methods). The beauty of this message is that for some, your name will stick in their head and they'll remember what it is that you do.

Perhaps then a post you put out, or video, will remind them and nudge them to get back to you.

3. The Problem Solver

> Hi (Insert Name),
>
> Thank you for connecting.
>
> I'd love to see if we may be able to help you (insert problem solved) with (insert product/service)?
>
> Kind Regards,
> Dan

This one is a step up from the introduction style post and goes in with a soft question essentially asking to talk. You thank them for connecting and then tell them how you would love to help them solve a particular problem with the product or service that you sell.

You ask in the form of a question so that those who have that problem and would like it solved are more inclined to then reply and open up the conversation.

This is a light message, quite soft and very simple. It's not packed with tonnes of features and benefits or a massive sales pitch, just a simple comment that you may be able to help them achieve something.

The type of replies it often generates are usually "yes I would be interested", often quite short but none the less it's an opening for you. I will then reply saying "That's great, what's the best email address and I'll pop you some more information on how we could help".

4. The Video Message

> Hi (Insert Name),
>
> If you can spare 3 minutes, here is a quick video of how we're helping similar companies to yours achieve (insert ROI) with (insert product) – (insert YouTube link or video)
>
> Kind Regards,
> Dan

Video is already an amazing sales tool and communication method, and LinkedIn gives you the opportunity to send video through message.

There are 2 ways you can do this, you can copy the link to a YouTube video or other hosted video, or you can attach it directly. These videos should be 2-3 minutes long max, and fully personalised. Ideally it will be a video of you talking to the prospect, almost like a video voicemail.

Make sure you're passionate about what you're saying, you need to be comfortable in front of the camera, so lots of practice first is highly recommended.

If you can, I'd highly recommend using subtitles/captions as well. A lot of people are using LinkedIn in a working office and so often can't actually listen to any content or video messages online. Having subtitles means they can still consume the video in their working day.

I use a platform called Zubtitle (other great ones are available as well). It's reasonably priced and super easy to use. You upload the video; it adds the captions, you check them to make sure they're right, and then you download it.

The big advantage of video is it's the closest thing to face to face interaction, which is the ultimate form of interaction you can have with a prospect. It's not just a voice over the phone or a piece of text in an email or message, it's actually you talking to them, looking into their eyes and telling them how you think you can help them.

BONUS TIP – *Use software like Vidyard which allows you to record a video of you whilst showing them something on your desktop screen. You could for example record it whilst on their LinkedIn profile explaining what makes you believe you can help them (their company, job title etc).*

They can see you, look into your eyes and see the confidence and passion that you have for your product, industry and for helping them. Make sure that passion and confidence is conveyed as if they were sat right in front of you.

It's the same principle as cold calling, to be effective you need to convey enthusiasm in your tone and voice. The best way to do that is to sit up straight or walk around while your talking, instead of slumped on your desk.

With video, sit up straight, keep strong eye contact and speak with confidence and passion to help ensure they feel confident in talking to you and potentially working with you in the future.

5. <u>Looking for Leadership Insight</u>

Hi (Insert Name),

I'm looking for some information from (insert industry) leaders around how they do (insert subject), would you be able to contribute?

Kind Regards,

Dan

A great way to get your foot in the door with a potential client is to ask for their thoughts, knowledge and experience.

This works very well for tough decision-makers, people who perhaps have quite small networks, or who have large networks but are very active on social. Sometimes this shows that they may have a bit of an ego and so asking for them to contribute feeds that.

Not only will you gather great information that will help you, but you'll also build a stronger foundation to the relationship compared to going straight in for the sale.

You can angle this around a specific blog that you're looking to write or even an industry whitepaper that your company is putting together. It feels great to be needed and to have your insights wanted for something relevant to the industry. I always get prospects jumping at the opportunity to contribute to something, to know their voice is valued.

I've done these many times over the years, and it's helped carve some very strong relationships and generate some very strong opportunities.

They feel appreciated and you've started the relationship in a much stronger way. You can use it to open up any number of conversations to explore their knowledge and experience, which will in turn uncover tonnes of valuable information that you can then leverage as a sales professional to provide an even better service to them.

When we feel like someone respects us, and when we have someone listen to us, we tend to like them and trust them. They're making effort, they're showing interest and these are perfect ways to start a buyer/seller relationship.

The more you know about them the better you can help them. This is a great chance to really practice active listening as well!

6. The Case Study Introduction

> Hi (Insert name),
>
> Last month we worked with (insert customer company). They spent X and achieved an ROI of (insert ROI). I've had a look through your profile, and I believe we may be able to help you achieve something similar, would it be possible to send you a little bit of information?
>
> Kind Regards,
> Dan

Another template very powerful with higher-level decision-makers, this one lays out not just an ROI, but evidence of how a company similar to theirs, and hopefully a company they will know or recognise has achieved it.

It's important that this is 100% proven and factual, and that you have a full case study or testimonial to send them if they ask.

This works by sparking interest in either the company that you mention or the ROI that they have achieved. This is a lot different from most of the messages that prospects will receive which are usually more focused on the salesperson and not the prospect.

This one is built for them, it's showing them that you have something that could and hopefully would benefit them, and you've got proof of how it has helped someone similar.

If you've got the case study available as a nice document you could even attach that to the message as well so they can open it and read the full thing, hopefully then giving them more confidence in you and growing their interest in what you're offering.

The reason this template can work really well is because we live in the "review buying" world.

Whenever we buy things online, we often look for reviews from people who have bought it before us. I do this myself, when I buy things online, like Amazon for example, I'll always read through the reviews. I bought a GoPro recently and spent ages reading through the reviews of various models, and those reviews influenced what I bought.

By using the case study message template you're showing them straight away that they can trust you and your company to deliver on what you're selling. You're showing them a real and positive result from buying from you, which will hopefully be from someone they know or may recognise.

Having numbers makes a big impact as well, if what you sell has a numerical impact. This will cut through the noise and ultimately get straight to the point with the prospect, which is what a lot of decision makers want at the end of the day.

Show them what you can help them achieve and show them why they should be open to talking to you.

This template has worked particularly well for me with very senior decision makers and C-Level decision makers, as it's to the point and backed up with real results.

7. The Free Trial or Demo Offer

Hi (Insert Name),

Are you looking to save money (or another ROI) on your (insert product)?

If so, I would love to help and offer you a free trial/demo of (insert product).

Kind Regards,

Dan

Many salespeople out there will offer a free trial or demo of their product to help get into a company, show them their product and increase their chances of then closing the deal.

This message is built to show them the potential ROI that they could achieve, and then offer them the opportunity to try before they buy.

You're ultimately trying to create a "what have you got to lose situation". Once they see that and hopefully agree, the free trial or demo then opens the door to the conversation and creates a sales opportunity for you.

This is a good message to send a few days after they accept your connection request, but certainly not 5 minutes after they accept! Try and engage with some of their content first and share some content of your own to provide some form of value before slipping into their LinkedIn DM's!

After you send it, if they don't reply, I would recommend following up with another LinkedIn message after a week or so.

Then, if they still don't reply, utilise other platforms such as the phone, email and post to ensure your message gets in front of them.

This template sometimes needs a little bit of follow up, but you've planted the seed of what your product does and shown them that they can try first. It's then just a case of working to get a conversation with them where you can explain more about the product and work to get them signed up.

Don't forget, whilst you wait for a reply and whilst you leverage other platforms like the phone and email etc, you can still leverage social selling.

Engage with their content to remind them that you are there and to get them more comfortable with your name. Also share your own content so that they start to receive value from you. If you give a good enough piece of content it can help encourage them to feel the need to reply to you.

Another great way to follow up on this is with the "Case Study Message Template". After you've pitched a free trial or demo, if they haven't replied send them a case study message, followed by informing them of the trial/demo at the end. This then gives them a reason to want to trial it with a result that will hopefully be appealing to them (which is should if you have correctly qualified them as a potential prospect.

8. The Event Invitation

> Hi (Insert Name),
>
> I'm running an event at (insert location) on (insert date) and thought it might be something that would interest you. Would you like a free ticket to attend?
>
> Kind Regards,
>
> Dan

Inviting someone to an event is a great way to prospect and create opportunities and inviting them via LinkedIn can be a powerful way to do it.

As we all know, most decision-makers receive hundreds of emails every day, so when you send them an invite via email, there is a high chance it will get ignored or sent to the spam folder.

Sending a nice short message like this inviting them often stands a higher chance of being seen and responded to. You can add a small amount of extra detail, perhaps mentioning what is going to be covered, for example, "We will have a Microsoft Expert in to discuss the latest technologies on the horizon".

If they reply, it's a win-win situation. If they say yes, it's a win, you get them to your event and have the opportunity to impress them and create an opportunity.

If they no it's still a win as they're now talking to you, you've opened the lines of communication. They'll either give you a reason, which will open up a warmer conversation.

If they just say no, a good way to try and keep the opportunity alive is to offer some form of industry research document, guide or eBook.

You're still offering something of value, knowledge and insight, but without the need for them to move past their computer. There is a decent chance they'll accept, and again, this creates the opportunity to talk.

You can follow up with a message after a few days asking if they had chance to read it or give them a call to discuss it.

Similar to the previous template this one is all about giving. The rule of reciprocity is very powerful in sales and by giving something it often makes them feel the need to give something back.

That might include a reply to your message or the acceptance of some information from you. Either way it helps increase your chances of opening the door with them.

I used to host events once a month or so and use one of our tech team to deliver a session of value that was attractive to our prospects. The only cost would be a few nibbles and drinks, which is a minimal cost in reality.

They then can come in, see our amazing workplace, meet us and build relationships with the opportunity to also qualify and book in a proper sales meeting.

9. Would You Like An eBook?

> Hi (Insert Name),
>
> We've just released a new eBook on the latest (insert industry) trends. Would you like a copy?
>
> Kind Regards,
> Dan

Following on from the previous template and the opportunity to send them an eBook, this message template offers that straight away. Perhaps you can't put on an event, or you'd like quicker results.

Offering them a strong piece of industry content is a really nice way to give something first and create a nice warm conversation starter.

If they say yes, then send it and similar to the message template above, follow up to discuss it a few days after. If they say no, perhaps look at sending the email directly with the content attached or even better, print it off and send it via post.

Not many decision-makers will receive something like that printed so it could make a good impact. Even if they say yes on LinkedIn, you could send them a digital copy and send a printed one as well for extra bonus points!

(It's all about standing out from the crowd, these templates will help digitally, but using post can really help as well).

An eBook or Guide only needs to be 10 pages long, ideally visually strong with some good valuable insight or knowledge within them.

If you have a marketing department, they should be able to create one quite easily if they don't already have some available.

If you don't have a marketing department, you'll be able to find plenty of free templates via Google or use Microsoft PowerPoint to create one and save it as a PDF copy to send.

Creating one isn't too difficult but if you're not feeling that creative or confident in doing so, look around your office for someone who may be able to help. If you don't have anyone, perhaps look at www.fiverr.com where you should be able to find someone able to do it for a very reasonable cost.

Use the knowledge and experience that you have, the knowledge and experience of your team and managers or use the insight you gained from asking other prospects or thought leaders for their input.

Try to find really engaging stand-out titles that will be as attractive as possible to your prospects. It needs to be a document that will make them want it, and ultimately be willing to talk/engage with you to receive it.

Whilst it may be tempting to use a click-bait style title, if you don't deliver in the eBook what you promised on the cover, you'll end up burning that bridge before you've even had a chance to walk across it. Create an engaging title that is then backed up by really strong content within the eBook, so your prospects feel they got value.

10. LinkedIn Recommended You

> Hi (Insert Name),
>
> You came up as a suggestion on LinkedIn today as someone I should connect with. I've had a look at your profile and think we may be able to help, we provide (insert product/service) to help companies like yours achieve (insert ROI).
>
> Would it be ok to send you some more information?
>
> Kind Regards,
>
> Dan

If you go into the "**My Network**" section on your LinkedIn profile, LinkedIn will give you a list of suggestions of people you could or should connect with. Within these lists are often prospects or people who work within prospective companies.

This is a nice template to use because it informs them that it was LinkedIn who recommended they connect, and as the platform that you're on, it's pretty trustworthy. Surely, they will trust LinkedIn?!

You then go on to find and give them the reason why the connection made sense and how you think you could help them. Have a look at their profile, qualify them as much as you can and find good reasons that you believe you could help them. It could be their position, company, company's current situation, just a bit of research should give you a good few opportunities to leverage.

The final part is to offer them some more information. You've told them LinkedIn recommends they connect; you're showing them you've made effort to research them and that you think you help them achieve something!

BONUS TIP – Alongside effective LinkedIn messaging I would highly recommend that you grow your network on a daily basis.

Using LinkedIn suggestions is a great place to start, and I would recommend adding at least 10+ people each day. I wouldn't add more than 25-35 per day because you'll increase the chance that LinkedIn will block your account for over adding.

This will help grow your network quicker, help grow your personal brand and potentially help you generate more sales opportunities as well.

If they don't reply, this will warm up the cold call a bit as you can reference the fact that LinkedIn recommended them to you and that after doing some research you believe that you may be able to help them.

You could also use this as an intro to a prospecting email, or even a prospecting letter. You could use it at a networking event or conference as well.

The key thing is that you're utilising LinkedIn as a micro-referral to help provide backing to your outreach to them.

11. Cards on The Table

> Hi (Insert Name),
>
> We have a (new) product (insert product) that does (insert solution). I'm confident we could help you achieve (insert potential ROI) with it, would it be possible to send you some more information?
>
> Kind Regards,
> Dan

Being honest and upfront can be a very powerful tool in sales. It's important to remember your prospects will be receiving tonnes of spammy sales messages on LinkedIn, via email and through cold calls every single day.

Very few will be upfront and honest that they're trying to sell something, they'll dance around it trying to craft messages that decision makers often see right through.

When a salesperson does put their cards on the table it can have a strong impact.

This message lays it all out nice and simple showing them what you offer and what it can help them achieve, and it shows them that you are honest and trustworthy.

It has got your product, an ROI and a solution, all of the core things you want them to understand that you offer. Play your cards on the table and let them see that you're not hiding anything or trying to deceive them.

12. The Shared LinkedIn Group

> Hi (Insert Name),
>
> We're both part of the (insert group name) group. I've actually been working with a few companies very similar to yours to help them with (insert problem solved or ROI). Would it be possible to send you some information on how we may be able to do the same for you?
>
> Kind Regards,
>
> Dan

I'll be very honest; groups on LinkedIn right now (2019) are not great. I live in hope that LinkedIn will breathe new life into them, taking some advice from Facebook where groups thrive.

However, I would never advise you to ignore them all together. There are still tonnes of groups out there, some with thousands, tens of thousands, even hundreds of thousands of members.

It can be very valuable joining industry groups and using the group as an introduction topic through messaging. Stating that you are in the same group of them will make you appear a lot warmer than just a cold salesperson. You could reference a recent piece of content shared in the group or look for some engagement and interaction that they've done and reference that.

BONUS TIP – Why not create your own industry group?! Build one that is totally neutral, so not associated with your company, and then invite as many of your prospects into it.

You can then control the content and use the group as a conversation starter with your prospects. Invite industry experts to contribute and build something that becomes a real value to everyone who is involved.

Make sure you're giving value every day in your group through content and content engagement. Groups require a lot of work but can create strong communities that can be leveraged to sell.

Another opportunity here is to go where groups really are thriving, Facebook. Connecting with prospects and customers on Facebook is a grey area. I have a handful of customers I am connected with on Facebook, and it helps take the relationship to a whole new level.

However, a lot of people like to keep it personal, which is absolutely fair enough.

Either way, you can still join industry groups and reference them on LinkedIn without actually connecting with them on Facebook directly. You can join them and start sharing content, which hopefully they will notice and start to be aware of your name and what you do.

Then when you approach them on LinkedIn they'll feel a lot warmer connecting with you and speaking with you, because you've already provided value.

13. Mutual Connection or Referral

> Hi (Insert Name),
>
> (Insert mutual connection/referral) suggested that I pop you a quick message as you may be able to benefit from what we offer here.
>
> We help people with our (insert product) to solve (insert problem). Would it be ok to send you a little bit of information about what we do?
>
> Kind Regards,
> Dan

Firstly, it is VERY important that if you are using this template, that you are **100%** positive that your prospect knows the person you're going to reference! I say this for one simple reason, just because someone is connected to someone on LinkedIn, it doesn't mean that they actually know them.

If I contacted a prospect and said, "John Smith suggested I pop you a message", and it turns out that my prospect has no idea who John Smith is, it backfires very quickly! LinkedIn might even be telling me that John Smith is a mutual connection; however, it doesn't mean that they actually know them.

This works well when you have a referral or have actually been recommended by a mutual connection to reach out.

If you're unsure, ask your mutual connection. Back to the example above, I could message John Smith and ask him whether he actually knows my prospect.

I could ask him to introduce me or even if he's not willing to do that, if I can confirm that he knows him I can use the above template.

When we reference someone they know, it helps break down some of the barriers that people put up when approached by a salesperson. By mentioning someone they know they start to look at you as a recommendation and not a cold salesperson.

BONUS TIP – If you do have a mutual connection or a customer who is making a referral, try to get it in writing. It could be within an email or a LinkedIn message.

Then you can copy and paste it and create a post, which you can send with this message template to actually prove it's a credible recommendation. This will help add some serious weight to what you're saying and increase the chance they respond.

Another helpful tip is to get your mutual connection to contact them as well. I'll ask the mutual connection to pop them an email explaining that they've passed their details to me, the reason why and also explaining why they thought it would be a good idea. This significantly increases the response rate as they'll be getting the recommendation directly from someone they know, like and should hopefully trust as well.

14. The Honesty Message

> Hi (Insert name),
>
> I'd love the opportunity to try to sell to you (insert product). I'm being completely honest here because I'm pretty confident that it's something that will help you. If afterwards you believe it's not right for you, then I'll happily leave you alone.
>
> Would it be possible to send you some information or give you a call later this week?
>
> Kind Regards,
> Dan

This is similar to the cards on the table message but taken a step further where you lay out from the start that you're trying to sell them something.

This same approach works well on cold calls as well where you open the call with admitting it is a cold call, and then you ask for 30 seconds to tell them what it is about, and if they're not interested you can leave it at that.

What you're doing is showing honesty from the start, but you're telling them you believe you can help them achieve something.

Because you've opened up with honesty, they're suddenly more likely to believe you when you tell them that you think you can help them.

It's one of the rare scenarios in sales where being honest that you're a salesperson actually helps BUILD trust!

You should never feel embarrassed to be a salesperson, embrace it and be proud in the fact that you are actually helping people achieve some pretty amazing things. When you're comfortable being a salesperson, being honest isn't a scary or daunting thing.

DON'T BE EMBARRASSED TO BE A SALES PROFESSIONAL...

BE PROUD!

HELLO my name is Dan and I'm a sales Professional!

YOU'RE [HELPING] PEOPLE
YOU'RE [SAVING] THEM MONEY
YOU'RE [SUPPORTING] THEIR BUSINESS

15. Did you get my letter...?

> Hi (Insert Name),
>
> I just wanted to see if you got my letter in the post?
>
> Kind Regards,
> Dan

Obviously, this template requires you to send a letter, but it creates another great opportunity to prospect.

Not many salespeople send letters anymore, so doing that in itself can be a powerful prospecting tool. Then following it up by messaging everyone you've sent letters to on LinkedIn can help increase conversions.

Let's say you sent 100 letters, and 10 got back to you. By contacting the other 90 via LinkedIn you could convert another 10+ prospect. It's important to keep the LinkedIn message super short and simple as this increases the chance that you'll get a reply.

It will encourage them to either acknowledge it, check to find the letter or tell you no in which case you can confirm details and send it again.

The letter could include a flyer or brochure, accompanied by a personalised letter explaining why you're sending it and why/how you think you can help them. Look for extra ways to make the letter stand out, like sending a tea bag and offering them a cuppa while they read it!

16. You're using our competitor

> Hi (Insert Name),
>
> I noticed on your website/our competitors' website that you're currently using (insert competitor).
>
> We offer a very similar product, but that has more features and at a more competitive price. Would it be ok to send you some information to see if you'd like to explore?
>
> Kind Regards,
> Dan

This is one of my favourite templates and one I've used many, many times. What I like a lot about this is that you're upfront and honest that they're using your competitor, but that you think you could offer them a better deal.

A lot of decision-makers, whilst sometimes on the front of it are loyal to their suppliers, are always keen to know what other options are out there.

They have numbers to hit as well, pressures and targets on them, and if you can get them closer to that than the company, they're currently using they're usually open to looking into it.

It's honest, but not in an aggressive or confrontational way, just simply stating that they clearly need what you sell, and your product might offer them more.

By showing that you know they're using a competitor, you're also showing them that you know they need what you sell. The challenge is to find an opportunity that you can offer more than your competitor. If you can't offer more, if your product is like for like with your competitor, then YOU need to be the difference.

In sales, YOU are just as important as the product you sell. People often buy into the person before they buy into the product.

This is when you need to really focus on building a strong relationship with them than they have with their current provider. A challenge, but not impossible and potentially very rewarding.

BONUS TIP – This is a great opportunity to leverage your personal brand (which obviously you have to build first). Share content every single day, engage in industry relevant content regularly and show yourself as a key person in the sector.

Check out the bonus chapters in this book for "Social Selling in 15 Minutes Per Day" for a super easy and time effective way to build a credible personal brand.

17. The ROI Question

> Hi (Insert Name),
>
> *If I could save you (insert ROI) on your (insert problem), would you be interested?*
>
> *Kind Regards,*
> *Dan*

Whilst the same in some ways to previous templates, this one is a little more to the point. You're asking them straight out that if you could achieve something for them would they be interested.

For example, going back to the previous example I used about the recruitment firm pitching to save up to 80% of recruitment costs would write something like this:

Hi John,

If I could save you 80% on your recruitment costs, would you be interested?

Kind Regards,

Dan

Imagine sending that to a hiring manager or business owner, who would be spending thousands, if not tens of thousands a year on recruitment costs. It's an attractive bait that will often generate a strong amount of bites with people replying, "yes, I would be interested".

This then opens the door for you to send information and start that all-important conversation.

You ideally, if possible, want to give them no reason to say no. You want to create the strongest possible value proposition, something that you know they will want.

I mean who wouldn't want to save 80% on their recruitment costs?!

That's the impact you want this message to have on the prospects that you send it to.

The other power of this particular message template is the pure simplicity of it. It is very short but very powerful. It's a message that they can read quickly and easily, which will help increase the chance that the reply.

As I mentioned at the start of this book, the key to effective LinkedIn messaging is to keep it short, sweet, light, and conversational. Cut through the noise of all the other long, boring and very sales focused messages with a simple powerful question like this.

Show them straight away that you potentially can help them achieve something and ask them if you could, would they be interested.

If you don't get a reply within a week or 2, follow it up with a cold call or email to elaborate further on how you can actually help them achieve that ROI with what it is that you are selling.

Sharing regular content that supports this will also help give soft nudges and encourage them to reply.

18. Recent Activity Observation

> Hi (Insert Name),
>
> I noticed today/yesterday/recently that you wrote about (insert recent post subject). This is something I've seen time and time again, you highlighted it perfectly; it was a really great post! What do you think (insert subject relevant question)?
>
> Kind Regards,
>
> Dan

When you visit your prospects LinkedIn profile, have a look at their recent activity and look for a piece of content that you can leverage to start a conversation.

That could be a post that they had written, a video they recorded, it could be a post following an industry event they went to or even a blog they shared or wrote.

The key is to compliment them on the post and then ask a question about the subject. Equally, if there is something you disagree with then feel free to challenge them on it (politely or professionally!). The aim is to encourage a response that you can then open the door of conversation.

It's a good opportunity for you to showcase your interest and knowledge of the industry and to start a neutral conversation based on a shared interest, not just you wanting to sell them something!

Messages like this template follow the theme of not trying to jump in bed with your prospect straight away.

BONUS TIP – Don't be a stalker! I've heard too many people referring to observing something on social media as stalking someone. Whilst this is funny within your friends, with prospects it's just a bit creepy and desperate.

My advice is to present it as "research" instead. This makes it look like effort instead of desperate sales tactics. It's 100% acceptable to research your prospects, to view their profiles and look through their activity. Just make sure you look at it as research and not stalking!

The other big strength of this template is that is has NOTHING to do with selling them something. You're just showing them that you're interested in what they are interested in and looking to discuss it further.

Yes, this is less direct, but it can be a much more effective way of getting your foot in the door, giving some value in the conversation and then earning the right to start to pitch what you're selling.

It's like business networking events. You don't go to them, walk up to someone and start pitching them. You ask them questions, find common interests and build rapport.

This template is very much on that level, network with prospects and play the long game to build strong and longer lasting relationships.

19. The Profile View

> Hi (Insert Name),
>
> I noticed today you viewed my profile OR Thank you for viewing my profile today. I'd love to know what your company is currently doing/using for (insert product/solution)?
>
> Kind Regards,
>
> Dan

This is another one of my favourite templates and one that has generated me a lot of revenue over the years. It's also one of the most under-used areas of social selling.

Every day people will be viewing your profile (they should if you're being active on LinkedIn). A percentage of those people will be prospects, and it's a huge opportunity for you to see when they've looked at your profile.

I'll share a case study I use in my training sessions that really brings this template to life:

After checking my profile views, which I do once or twice a day, I noticed that the Managing Director and Sales Director of the same company had viewed my profile.

Now I sell 3 things personally, LinkedIn/Social Selling Training, Keynote Speaking and Advertising for The Daily

Sales. I could quickly see by looking at their profiles that this would be a potential interest in LinkedIn/Social Selling.

It had been 3 hours since they had both viewed my profile, and I hadn't received a LinkedIn message from them or an email.

What had happened, which I later found out, was that they were having their regular weekly meeting, and the topic of social selling came up. Both of them were connected to me on LinkedIn and had seen my content and activity. They discussed potential training and then moved on to the many other things to discuss about the business.

Now clearly it wasn't a pressing need at that time for them to reach out to me, perhaps they would have done later that day, later that week, maybe even later that month.

We all know what it's like, we discuss tonnes of these things daily, but they often sit on the back burner.

Anyway, after noticing that they had viewed my profile, and qualifying them as a potential prospect, I sent them both a LinkedIn message following this exact template.

I had a reply within 10 minutes from the Managing Director. It read:

"Thanks for your message Dan, yes we were discussing this today. We currently use LinkedIn a bit, but we would be interested to see if there is more, we could do with it. Could you speak to my Sales Director to explore?"

He helped me arrange a phone call, which led to 3 phone calls, 2 face to face meetings and one lunch before they hired me to train their company.

Now, they may have reached out to me, but as a true hunter sales professional, I don't want to leave things like this to chance. That could have taken weeks, months or longer, and all that time one of my competitors could have approached them and won the opportunity.

Ensure you check your profile views regularly, qualify those that could be prospects and use that profile view as the opportunity to start a conversation.

The template here is light and conversational but it shows them that you are totally in control of your business, that you're pro-active and that you're keen to help them.

This is a very strong way to start the relationship with a prospect and lays some very strong foundations as well.

BONUS TIP – *Obviously it is very important that you have the strongest possible LinkedIn profile so that when they do view it, they are interested in talking to you and potentially buying from you.*

A strong LinkedIn profile needs to have a good profile photo, background image, strong summary and a decent amount of recommendations (as well as all of the other sections of the profile as well).

Check out the bonus chapters for one on how to build a strong LinkedIn profile, it covers the basics but is a good place to start in creating a better profile.

20. The Direct Profile View Message

> Hi (Insert Name),
>
> I noticed you viewed my profile today, are you possibly looking at (insert product/solution)?
>
> Kind Regards,
> Dan

A more direct version of the profile view message, instead of asking loosely what they're doing relevant to your product/industry, this one goes straight to the question of whether they are looking specifically for what it is you sell.

I'd recommend only using this one once you've qualified that they could be a potential prospect.

If you haven't and they don't have any relevant need then it becomes a spam message and one that can burn a bridge from someone who might introduce you to a customer in the future.

I occasionally use this one after a few days of the profile view (changing the **today** part) and use it as a follow-up message for those that haven't replied.

Going back to the profile view example I shared earlier, I'm pretty confident that this message would have worked with them as well and would have generated a reply. The key is to make sure that you qualify them first to make sure there is a potential match there.

21. The Engagement Thank You

> Hi (Insert Name),
>
> Thank you for liking my recent blog/post/video on LinkedIn! What were your thoughts on (insert content topic)?
>
> Kind Regards,
>
> Dan

In a similar context to your profile views, the engagement on the content you share and create is another fantastic door opening opportunity.

Once again let me bring this particular template to life with a case study:

When I was selling in the IT sector, I had not long started writing my own sales blog on LinkedIn as well. I'd publish an article a week on sales via LinkedIn, and they would gain some average engagement each time.

Obviously, whilst sharing these blogs, I was looking to reach IT Managers and IT Directors of small to medium-sized companies.

One company in particular that I was prospecting to was proving very tough to get through. I'd tried cold calling multiple times, left voicemails, sent emails; I just couldn't get the attention of the decision-maker (something I'm sure a lot of salespeople will relate to).

After sharing another one of my sales blogs one week, I noticed that one of the sales reps at that company had clicked like on my article. Nothing else, no comment or share, just a simple like.

I realised that whilst not the decision-maker themselves, they could hold the key to the decision-maker. I sent them a LinkedIn message following the template above. The salesperson replied straight away and over a few messages we discussed the topic of the blog.

After building some rapport, I had earned the opportunity to mention what I was selling. I then had the chance to send this message:

"Actually, I wonder if you could help me? I've been trying to speak to your IT Manager about what we sell but am struggling to get through to them!"

The salesperson was more than happy to help, providing me with an internal introduction and arranging a phone call with them.

I then used that phone call to book a face to face meeting and turned that into a confirmed sale.

Now a big part of utilising this particular message template is the requirement for you to share or create content that drives engagement.

Unfortunately, there is so much to this which I physically can't fit into this book! If you're interested in learning how to create the best possible content on LinkedIn have a look at the content I share.

You will see that I follow a very strong set of content templates that I've mastered over the years which allow me to create content that generates such strong engagement numbers. Whether it is a post, article or video, they all follow a very similar format.

You'll get a good idea of what those templates look like and how you can start to use them for your own content.

TOP TIP – When creating content, share your stories. It could be stories from your past or present but share stories that overall have a positive message. The key is to show your prospects that you have knowledge, insight and experience. It's also important to show them YOU as a human being, and not just another salesperson.

Show them that you work hard, that you're dedicated, that you have challenges but that you work relentlessly hard to overcome them. Make it relevant to them and valuable to them in some form. Perhaps it's entertaining, perhaps it's motivational or perhaps it's educational.

To benefit from using this template, your content needs to be good enough to drive engagement. It needs to be as valuable to your prospect as possible and written in a way that encourages people to engage. Think about asking questions or creating debate to drive more people to engaging with it.

22. Going to the same event

> Hi (Insert Name),
>
> I noticed that you are going to (insert event) next week. I'm going to be there as well and would love the opportunity to buy you a coffee. Do you have any free time in the morning or afternoon?
>
> Kind Regards,
>
> Dan

OR

> Hi (Insert Name),
>
> Next week is the (insert industry event), and I wondered if you were planning to attend?
>
> Kind Regards,
>
> Dan

Attending key events is a core part of networking and prospecting for many salespeople.

Messaging prospects beforehand can be a great way to book in meetings at the event before it happens, helping increase your chances of success.

There are 2 ways to utilise this message:

The first is if you know that they are attending. Perhaps their company posted that they were attending or perhaps they posted about it on their feed.

Either way, if you know, they're attending you have an opportunity to invite them for a coffee or lunch to chat with you whilst you're there.

The other way is assuming you don't know if they're attending an event or not. You can use this opportunity to message them and ask if they were planning to attend.

If they are, you'll know and then be able to ask if they'd like to grab a coffee. If they weren't attending, you've bought the event to their attention, showing that you are immersed in your industry.

If you or your company are actually exhibiting at an event, this can also be a great template to help book some warm meetings with potential prospects. Invite them to your stand for a free coffee and quick catch up.

I see a lot of companies pay thousands to exhibit at an industry event, yet their salespeople just hide behind the stand and never go to actually speak to people (they'll often then complain that the event was bad when in fact they just didn't approach it in the right way).

One way to help push past that is to pre-arrange meetings with prospects by using this message template. You can also post about the event on LinkedIn and ask whether anyone in your network is there, then messaging those that are.

23. The Sharing Content Message

> Hi (Insert Name),
>
> I've just published an article/post/video on LinkedIn on your industry (insert industry), I'd love to know your thoughts –
>
> Kind Regards
>
> Dan

Giving value in a message is another great way of starting a conversation, such as by sharing a piece of content that you think they will enjoy or benefit from.

I must stress you need to make sure the first time you use this on a prospect that the content you choose to share with them is a good as possible.

If you send them something that isn't good, you'll decrease the chance they'll read something else from you, or actually respond/reply to the message itself. It needs to be a brilliant stand-out piece of content that is packed with as much value for them as possible.

Find or create an amazing piece of content that is absolutely packed with value for them and send it. You can expand this message a little bit to describe what's included in the piece of content or why you think it would be valuable to them to try and increase the chance that they will actually read the content that you have sent them.

For example:

I've just published an article of the top 5 tools that help increase social selling results. One of these tools will find the best industry content for you and gives you the chance to share it to your network with just a simple text.

You're giving them value, showing your knowledge and giving them a reason to actually read it as well.

The aim is to get them to read/watch/listen to the content so that you can then use it to then create a conversation. With the right content, you should also be able to make a good first impression with them and potentially build the layers of trust as well.

TOP TIP – When writing and publishing a LinkedIn article, try to keep it to 1000 – 1200 words, this is the optimum length. One of the most important factors of a successful article is the title. It needs to be bold, to stand out and to really make them want to read it.

It's also important to have a strong blog image and include media within the blog to break up the text and make it easier to read. Use www.canva.com to make easy and perfect LinkedIn blog images.

As a final tip I'd also highly recommend including spaces between sentences and paragraphs. It makes it a lot easier to read when scrolling down and will increase the chance that people read more of it.

24. The Research Message

> Hi (Insert Name),
>
> I don't want to waste your time, but I've done some research on you and (insert their company) and believe we could help you achieve (insert ROI).
>
> Could I send you a quick email and if it's something you're potentially interested in perhaps we could jump on a call?
>
> Kind Regards,
> Dan

What works really well with this template is the fact you are showing effort; you are showing them that you have done research and believe you can help. A lot of salespeople, especially in years gone by, would just phone cold data from a spreadsheet.

They would have no idea who they were phoning or whether that person would benefit. What this template does is do the opposite; it shows them that you HAVE researched them and believe you can actually help them.

I must stress that this isn't one that can be copied, pasted and sent to everyone in your network. You actually do have to research them, qualify them and have a good reason for wanting to message them. It can help to reference something specific that backs up and proves that you have done the research which will help encourage a reply.

The best salespeople out there know that there are no shortcuts to success in sales. No amount of copying and pasting or faking things in sales will help make things work quicker or easier.

As they say…

There is no elevator to the top in sales, you have to climb the stairs.

It's worth that extra effort thought trust me, this is how you stop wasting time trying to sell to anyone and everyone and start investing your time talking to the right people more likely to actually convert into sales.

BONUS TIP – One way to really support this message template is to view their profile.

Some prospects will and do check their profile views, and if they see that you've viewed their profile, they will know that you have actually been researching them.

Some people feel it looks bad to view a prospects profile, but I think it can be seen in a positive way, which I think this message template does.

25. The Missed Call Message

> Hi (Insert Name),
>
> I tried to call you today, but you were busy. I noticed on your profile that you are the (insert job title) at (insert company). I believe we may be able to help you achieve (insert ROI) and wondered if I could send you some more information by email?
>
> Kind Regards,
>
> Dan

The power of this one is that it shows you made an effort and tried to phone them.

For a lot of people, this is the sign of a strong salesperson and not just someone sending spammy messages one after the other. I must say that it is very important that you **ACTUALLY** do try to call them!

I can imagine some salespeople trying to "hack" their way with this, send loads of LinkedIn messages saying they tried to call and then when the prospect checks and finds out they didn't actually call, create a bigger problem!

For a lot of you reading this book, you will already be making tonnes of cold calls each day and following each of those up on LinkedIn with a message like this could really help. It may even help convert more of those calls into opportunities instead of just losing them.

If you're not keen on cold calls, perhaps you're a little scared or just lack a bit of confidence, I want you to remember one little thing…

DON'T FEAR THE PHONE…… IT MAKES YOU MONEY!

— Daniel Disney

The phone makes you money!

Social Selling works best when you use it WITH the phone and with email, and with all of the other amazing platforms and tools out there.

I don't think there is any chance that I could have closed the Million-Pound sale without the phone. I needed it to qualify them properly, to arrange a face to face meeting, to ask questions, to build rapport and more.

There you go, 25 tried, tested and proven LinkedIn message templates for you to use. Use the wisely, use them properly and go out there not to simply sell a product, but to help someone solve a problem.

What If They Don't Reply?

What If They Don't Reply?

No strategy in sales works 100% of the time; most work at a relatively low percentage of conversion. Cold calling tends to yield a 1-4% success rate, with the majority never turning into anything. With messaging on LinkedIn, you will get people that don't reply (if you've worked in sales for more than 1 day, you'll be used to this!).

So, what happens if they don't reply then?

Let me share a quick story of where this really came to life.

I was booked to deliver training with a company. Whilst doing some final preparation a week before, I noticed someone in my own personal LinkedIn network share a post asking for a recommendation for the exact same product that the company I was due to train was selling.

I had a good relationship with the director, so I tagged them into the post saying that I would personally recommend their company.

The week passed, and the day came where I travelled to deliver their 1-Day LinkedIn Masterclass. As the team arrived into the training room, one of the delegates came up to me and said they had seen the post which I tagged their director in.

They went on to tell me that they don't believe their director had noticed nor reacted to it, so they took the pro-active approach to comment, connect and message with the prospect themselves.

"That's brilliant," I said! *"What happened next,"* I asked?

"Well, I'm just waiting for them to reply to my message," they told me…

I paused, looking slightly confused…

"I'm sorry, what? You're <u>WAITING</u> for them to reply?"

The room went silent…

"Yes", they said, only now starting to doubt their logic.

I went on to explain to them how posts like this generate easily over 100 likes, comments and messages to the prospect. Their LinkedIn inbox will be FULL of messages from salespeople trying to win their business. The likelihood of them replying, unfortunately, is often very low.

This is one of the biggest missed opportunities in social selling, sitting there waiting for replies.

I can guarantee you at least 80% of the salespeople that comment on these posts or send LinkedIn messages rarely use other tools as well.

They also just sit there and wait, in fact, there is a chance that as you're reading this now, you've acknowledged that you fall into that trap as well. Don't worry if that's the case; we all have to learn somehow!

And this is where this section comes into play…

What if they don't reply?

Well if they don't reply, **PICK UP THE PHONE!!**

Pick up that wonderful phone and give them a call. Wait, what if they don't answer? Well don't get me wrong, there is also, a very low chance of them answering your call. If they don't answer, send them an email.

The Sad Truth of Sales In 2019

Sales Manager: Give them a call
Sales Rep: I've emailed them
Sales Manager: Be quicker to call them...
Sales Rep: I've texted them as well
Sales Manager: JUST CALL THEM
Sales Rep: I'll send another email

JUST PICK UP THE PHONE AND CALL!

If they don't reply to your email, send them a letter. Then, after a few days, give them a call again. Perhaps try and engage with their content, like a post, write a comment, let them know that you're there.

Keep trying as much as you can.

You need to remember one important thing…

YOU ARE A SALESPERSON!

Your job is to hunt, to go out, find, create and close sales opportunities.

Real salespeople don't wait around; they try everything in the power to go out there and help people with their product or service.

So, if your prospect doesn't reply to your message, don't wait around, start using other platforms that sit there at your disposal.

Salespeople need to use the modern-day sales toolkit to truly succeed...

THE MODERN DAY SALES TOOLKIT

DANIEL DISNEY
13.06.18

Use all of these tools and the many others including post, text, face to face, there will probably still be people using fax out there! The more tools that you have on your belt, the more tools you know and have mastered, the more opportunities you'll create to generate more pipeline and close more deals.

The true modern sales master has a well-equipped belt.

Pick Up the Phone

Pick Up the Phone

Yes, you are reading this right, a LinkedIn book written by a social seller has a chapter called "Pick up the phone"!

I've spent over 10 years making, training and leading large sales teams making cold calls. Whilst I now focus on helping salespeople leverage LinkedIn, I know the power and importance of the phone and am certainly not scared to pick it up and use it.

There's an unfortunate stigma in social selling that most social sellers are too scared to pick up the phone and want to just hide behind a computer.

Whilst I don't doubt there are people out there scared to use the phone to sell, it's certainly not just social sellers nor is social selling the reason that salespeople don't use the phone.

It has never been "**social selling VERSUS cold calling**", whilst the debate rages on in sales it's never been about choosing one or the other. Ultimately if you choose, you lose.

Here's a simple truth that I need you to know:

Some of your prospects will ONLY buy from you if you phone them.

Think back to the modern-day prospecting maze that I showed you earlier in this book, and what I said about communication preferences. There are many people out there who prefer to use the phone, who prefer to buy or discuss buying over the phone.

This book will hopefully show you how to leverage LinkedIn messaging to generate opportunities and communicate with prospects and customers, but it works EVEN better alongside the phone.

You can use LinkedIn messages to arrange phone calls, generate interest, confirm meetings, send information, follow up, and so much more.

If you are scared of making cold calls, or if you're trying to justify to yourself that they don't work, perhaps you don't like them, or think that they're dead, I would take a minute and just challenge yourself.

Put your hands up and admit that chances are, some of your prospects and customer ARE using the phone and that using it yourself COULD help you sell more.

All you're doing by avoiding using the phone is missing out on a number of potential customers that will only ever buy from you if you use the phone.

Don't miss out, pick up that phone, feel confident that you're trying to help them achieve something, then just pick up that phone, smile and dial 😊.

Next Steps

Hopefully, in this book, you'll have learned how you can leverage LinkedIn messages to start more conversations, create more opportunities, build more pipeline and hopefully generate more sales.

The first next step is to go and use what you've learned!

After that, I hope you then look to start using all of the other ways you can leverage LinkedIn to sell. These include:

- **Your LinkedIn Profile**
- **LinkedIn Searches**
- **Your Personal Brand**
- **Sharing Content**
- **Creating Content**

All of this is covered in my LinkedIn Social Selling Online Masterclass and 1-Day Live Workshop.

However, I want to give you a few top tips right now as a thank you for buying this book to help you get started.

I've added in several BONUS CHAPTERS which are packed with social selling tips, how to build a strong LinkedIn profile and more.

Read through them, implement them into your sales routine and you'll be well on your way to becoming a Social Selling master!

BONUS CHAPTERS

BONUS CHAPTER 1 – Social Selling Top Tips

Messaging on LinkedIn is a big part of Social Selling, but there are so many ways that you can leverage it to create and close sales opportunities. To get you started on your Social Selling journey, here are a few of my top tips:

1) Create Your Own Billboard LinkedIn Profile Banner

One of the most wasted opportunities within LinkedIn is your profile banner. Most salespeople either have it blank or with a very bland generic/corporate image. The reality is this is the perfect space to have your own personal billboard! It's one of the first things your prospects will see, and so it's a great opportunity, in as few words as possible, to try to tell them what you offer.

2) Write an Elevator Pitch Style Profile Summary

Most of us know the elevator pitch principle, the idea that if you were in an elevator with a prospect, what would you say in 30 seconds that would tell them what it is you do and give them a reason to be interested. Well, your LinkedIn profile summary is now your modern-day digital elevator pitch.

It's often the first thing people will read and learn about you. My top tip is to make it customer-focused, don't write about how great you are at selling, but write about how great you are at helping people.

3) Comment on Relevant Posts Every Single Day.

You don't need to spend more than 5-10 minutes per day, commenting on at least 2-3 posts, to make an impact. Make sure the posts you comment on are industry relevant.

Some may be the posts shared by your prospects, some may be posts shared by key industry people or other people that work in your prospects' company. Those comments will help build your personal brand and get your name known with your prospects, making for warmer introductions.

4) Write a Post Every Single Day

This shouldn't take any more than 5-10 minutes each day but is one of the quickest and best ways you can build a personal brand and generate sales opportunities. The posts should be valuable to your prospects and network.

You can tell stories, share experiences, ask questions, start debates, just use it as an opportunity to give value to your audience and open the doors to you, let them see and get to know you as a real human being. Make them easier to read when people are scrolling by including a clear space between sentences and paragraphs.

5) Share videos on LinkedIn

Recording and sharing a video on LinkedIn isn't the easiest thing to do, trust me when I started recording videos of myself; it was one of the toughest things I've ever done! I used to hate holding my phone in front of my face and talking to myself for a few minutes; it was even worse watching it afterwards.

However, video is one of the most powerful forms on content on LinkedIn, and it's growing day by day. Try sharing a few videos each month, no more than 2-3 minutes each, with subtitles/captions, on valuable content for your prospects.

One of my top tips when recording videos is to imagine that you're just talking to someone. Imagine your prospect is sat in front of you or that you're talking to them via a video call.

This can help remove the weirdness of talking to yourself and also help you present yourself in a professional way.

6) Customize your LinkedIn profile URL

Another super simple but effective tip is to customize your LinkedIn profile URL code. When you set up your profile, it will automatically give you a URL that will be full of random numbers and letters, which isn't easy to share.

If you go into your profile and look at the top right-hand corner, you should see the option to "Edit public profile & URL". Click that, and at the top right-hand corner of that page, you'll see the option to edit your URL. For example, mine is now www.linkedin.com/in/danieldisney

7) Add a link to your profile in your email signature

This is such a simple but powerful tip, add a link to your LinkedIn profile into your email signature. You can just write the link in, or it's pretty easy to add in a LinkedIn logo that links through (just search Google for LinkedIn email signature).

It means that everyone you email (which I'm sure is tonnes of people!) will be directed to your profile. This will help you grow your audience and potentially help you grow relationships with prospects and customers. It's also a nice modern professional addition to your signature.

8) Use the Top Industry Hashtags in Your Content

Hashtags are growing on LinkedIn and in 2019 LinkedIn announced that content performance would be impacted a lot more by the correct use of hashtags.

Find 2-3 of the best performing key hashtags in your posts, try not to use any more. This is where Twitter can come in handy as it will show you what are the top trending hashtags right now. These could be great ones to use or great subjects to write about.

You could also look at creating your own hashtag so people can follow your posts. Try to keep them simple and consistent.

BONUS CHAPTER 2 – How to Build A Great LinkedIn Profile

Most salespeople, when going into a customer-facing environment, whether it's a face to face meeting, a skype call or a networking event, will dress as smart as possible.

They'll put on nice suits, nice dresses, nice shoes, jewellery, accessories, nice hair, make-up etc. They'll spend lots of money on clothes, shoes, watches, everything needed to look smart.

They'll make a significant effort to look as good as possible for their prospects or customers, to make a good impression.

What you don't see is businesses and sales professionals having the same attitude towards their DIGITAL appearance.

Not only do we have a physical presence to think about, we now have a DIGITAL presence to consider as week,

In fact, for some of you out there, MORE of your prospects and customers will see you DIGITALLY than physically!

We now need to start applying the same thought process that we have for our physical self and start applying it more to our digital self as well. Our social media profiles, personal brands and digital footprint.

For some of your prospects their first impression of you will be your LinkedIn profile, which is why it's so important that it's the best it can possibly be.

Here's a little doodle I did to illustrate this...

DRESSING SMART NOW INCLUDES HAVING A GOOD SOCIAL MEDIA PROFILE!

The reality is that there are probably more prospects and customers looking at your social profiles than looking at you face to face. Your social profile should look just as good as you do, and you should invest just as much time as you would in your physical appearance.

With that in mind, here are the basic steps needed to create a strong LinkedIn profile:

Before we jump into each section, one thing to always remember with your LinkedIn profile is to think about your target audience.

If you're trying to get a job, for example, then your profile should all be about why someone should interview or employ you. If you're looking to prospect and sell through LinkedIn, then your profile needs to all be about the value you offer.

The way to look at it is to imagine your dream prospect visiting your page right now. What would they need to see to feel comfortable in talking to you and potentially buying from you? Every part of your profile should be built to help your prospect get to know and trust you to then give you the opportunity to progress that relationship.

Let's break down each section of your LinkedIn profile...

Profile Photo - Let's start with one of the most important components of your profile, your profile picture. I've seen some great ones, and not so great ones over the years. I know it's not always easy finding a suitable smart photo to use, which is why I often see photos from weddings (often the last time a nice photo was taken when you were dressed smart!).

The reality is now that most people reading this will have a smartphone with a pretty powerful camera, so next time you're in the office get a colleague to take a decent headshot against a plain background and boom, perfect profile picture!

Nothing will be better than a professionally taken profile photo though. My photo was done by the extremely talented David Green from **"Shoot Me Now"**. I honestly wouldn't recommend anyone else, check him out at **www.shootmenow.co.uk**.

Background Image - Behind your profile photo is space for a background image to be loaded up. Please don't ignore this part; it's fine to choose a plain background or upload a generic one; however, you can create a custom one for free using Canva (www.canva.com). You can include your company logo or mission statement or even your contact details. Something that looks smart looks on brand and captures attention.

The goal is to show them what you do in as simple a way as possible. You want them to look at it and hopefully know what it is your offer and how it may apply to them.

Headline - The next step is the headline. This is often just populated with your job title, which is fine; however, you can be a little more creative and make it more about what you do or what you can offer.

For me, I use LinkedIn to grow my personal brand, so my headline talks about me, but you might want to discuss what you offer or a reason as to how you can help your target customer.

One of the most popular formats that I recommend is the "Helping people achieve X with Y" or the "Providing X to Y to help achieve ROI".

Summary Section - This section is your opportunity to give a nice elevator pitch summary of you, what you do and what you can offer. Mine highlights a summary about me, what I can offer, achievements that help prove my ability to deliver and my contact details. Now I know your contact details are available on your profile, but you should want them to be as clear as possible so popping them into the summary box helps make them even more visible.

BONUS TIP - *You can attach media to your summary and work experience. This can be an image, blog, video, website, presentation or link and is a great way to provide some extra media highlighting what you and offer.*

Articles & Activity - This will show all of your activity as in posts you click like, comment on, or share. This section will also show the articles/blogs that you write on LinkedIn. This is another place your prospect may look so it's important to be aware of what content you like and how you engage as your prospects may see it.

Work Experience - This section is for you to list your past and current work experience. Less is often more in these sections but give your prospect the opportunity to see what experience you have and how it may relate to your ability to provide value to them.

This is also a good place to include a little more about your current company and what makes them different/unique. There is also the ability to add media so you can link the company website, include your sales pitch presentation, a video, media that will help the prospect buy into what you do.

Featured Skills & Endorsements - This is one of the real stand-out features of LinkedIn as both fantastic recruitment platform and a fantastic sales platform. In this section, potential buyers can see areas where you have been endorsed by other people.

For example, if you were selling software and your prospect could see you've been endorsed for "Software", "Account Management", "Customer Service" etc. by plenty of people it helps them feel more comfortable buying from you.

BONUS TIP – You can choose which 3 sit at the top of the list and so are the most visible. Click the edit item to move them around and into place.

Recommendations - Taking it one step further, not only can people endorse you for skills, but they can write a full personal recommendation!

Imagine again that you're selling software and your prospect visits your profile and sat, there are several recommendations from other software companies talking about how much you helped them, saved them money, listened to them etc.

BONUS TIP - Just as I'm sure you'll have a referral process in place to get referrals and case studies from your customers, create one to get recommendations on your LinkedIn profile as they are just as powerful.

Accomplishments - This is a great opportunity to list any courses, certifications or awards that you've received. Again, imagine your prospect viewing your profile and being able to see what you are qualified in. It adds some real power to how you are seen.

Interests - You might not think this would interest a prospect, but imagine they looked at this part and saw that you were interested in key industry companies or pages.

It would show them that you're interested in what they are interested in and that you had a real genuine interest.

EXTRA Quick Profile Tips

- Keep it up to date, make sure you're updating it regularly
- Create a simple personalised URL link for your LinkedIn profile (go to the top right-hand corner, click "Edit public profile & URL" and then look at the top right-hand corner again to change it.
- Add that link into your email signature

Follow these tips, fill in each section, make sure it flows nicely, looks professional and at every stage, make sure you think about how your customer will feel reading it.

BONUS CHAPTER 3 – Cold Calling Is Just Like Blockbuster

I've talked a bit about cold calling this book, and hopefully, you'll see that I'm very

So why Blockbuster? It is because it went bust. Am I just saying cold calling is dead? NO!

In my opinion, Blockbuster should still be alive and thriving today in the same way that a lot of cold callers are thriving today.

What Blockbuster highlights change, and how refusing to change or adapt is a risky way to approach business. Blockbuster ended as a business because they didn't adapt quick enough to evolve with the rest of the industry. Whilst new businesses were coming up with streaming services, which were growing really fast, Blockbuster refused to adapt and kept pushing the "film rental" market.

Technology advanced, and people were now able to watch films on demand, when they want with no late fees!

Now if Blockbuster had adapted and launched a streaming service, they could still be going (and growing) today. Blockbuster had a huge brand known all over the world for films, and they could have easily built and grown a streaming brand in the same way Netflix have.

They could have kept the stores going as people still like to shop and would still rent newly released movies that aren't available on Netflix or streaming sites.

This is EXACTLY the situation that cold calling is in right now!

Cold calling is a prospecting activity that thrived when the phone was our main source of communication. Just like Blockbuster thriving when the only way we could watch films was to buy or rent them via video or DVD.

Just like the world of streaming and downloading interrupted the film industry, other forms of communication such as social media, instant messaging, email and video, are now interrupting the prospecting and sales industry.

If you refuse to adapt and evolve, if you think the phone will always be the main form of communication and that nothing will change, you stand a high chance of ending up like Blockbuster, out of business.

I'm not saying that the phone will die, like I said at the start people still buy and watch DVD's in the same way people still use the phone now and will continue to do so for years to come.

However, people are now communicating more via social media, instant messaging, email and video. Now is the time adapt these new methods, learn them properly and master them.

Blockbuster, Toys R Us, it's the same story......

In the UK a few weeks ago it was announced that Toys R Us, a popular toy shop, was closing down. Most people jump on this to blame websites such as Amazon which certainly contribute to this.

However, in the same way, Blockbuster could still be thriving today so could Toys R Us! If they had adapted with the changing way people buy and embraced the online world of purchasing, they could again still be thriving.

The salespeople and sales teams that have embraced social selling, email, messaging and video are thriving today. They've grown their pipelines, increased their sales and grown their business. Suddenly they're able to reach more people and have more conversations.

What should you do?

If you are ONLY cold calling now is the time to really wake up to the fact that this is not a strong sales strategy. You're missing out on loads of opportunities to generate sales opportunities via social media, email, video and instant message. It's not about replacement but utilising it ALONGSIDE cold calling.

The phone will continue to be a strong source of prospecting, but there are A LOT of people using or more responsive to other platforms. Be smart, be proactive and use them all!

Just don't be like Blockbuster…

Scared to change, scared to adapt and scared to evolve. Embrace the change, OWN the change and become the person who is AHEAD of the change.

Accept that your prospects and customers are using social media as well as the phone and start using them together to win.

DON'T BE LIKE [BLOCKBUSTER] SCARED TO CHANGE

Be a survivor in sales, adapt to the changing landscape, embrace new methods, new platforms and new techniques.

Practice them, master them and start generating more sales with them. That's the real recipe for success in sales.

BONUS CHAPTER – Social Selling in Just 15 Minutes Per Day

Salespeople are busy, fact.

Between making hundreds of cold calls, attending countless team meetings, sending emails, sending proposals, closing deals, overcoming objections, the list goes on.

When you then have people telling you that you need to do social selling now as well, where on earth are you going to find time to do that?!

Are you really supposed to spend hours each day on LinkedIn?

Luckily the answer is no!

In this chapter, I want to help show you how you can achieve social selling results from as little as just 15 minutes each day. Surely everyone reading this can find 15 minutes each day. Especially if those 15 minutes had the potential to generate you MORE sales?

But Dan, there's no way I can achieve anything in just 15 minutes?

I actually mentioned this on a webinar recently, and a couple of the attendees pushed back and said that wasn't possible.

Don't get me wrong; if you can and want to invest more time into social selling, you'll obviously have the opportunity to generate more results.

However, as many salespeople and sales leaders are often crazy busy as it is, I wanted to find a way that with as little time as possible they could leverage LinkedIn way better and start generating results.

Let me show you how...

To really see results, I've broken the 15 minutes into 3 X 5-minute activities. To see results, they really need to be on a regular, consistent daily basis. That's part of why this can work.

1 - Grow Your Network (5 Minutes)

The first stage is to start growing your network each and every day. Spend the first 5 minutes adding potential prospects, adding people within prospective companies or adding people relevant to your industry.

LinkedIn will automatically recommend people for you, or you can do a couple of quick searches.

If you can add at least 10 connections each day, that's 300 each month and 3600 in a year. If you're slowly filling your network with prospects, you'll then increase the chance of generating inbound enquiries plus you'll create the opportunity to start outbound conversations with them via messaging.

2 - Share & Create Content (5 Minutes)

5 minutes isn't a lot of time in the world of content, but it's enough to start.

My advice would be to subscribe to as many industry-relevant new channels as possible. This way, you'll get the latest industry news direct to your inbox every day. Finding a good article and clicking the LinkedIn icon to share takes a couple of minutes, plus adding your own thoughts takes you up to the 5.

Creating a nice post can easily be done in 5 minutes. Whether it's a quick photo of yourself in a specific location with some writing attached, a quick story, some insight or even a short 3-minute video, you can easily create something impactful in 5 minutes.

I would advise that you share 2 bits of news each week and create 3 posts each week.

By sharing content every day, you'll start to build a personal brand. People will get used to seeing your name and will associate it with value and knowledge.

Done right, your content has the potential to generate inbound leads, and you have the opportunity to use the engagement or content to start conversations with prospects.

3 - Social Post Engagement (5 Minutes)

The final 5 minutes should be invested in social engagement. This includes everything from liking a few posts and commenting on a few posts.

This should be a mixture of engaging on your prospects content but also on industry-relevant content.

The aim is to make sure your name is out there every day. By engaging on your prospect's posts, you'll earn credibility, build relationships and hopefully generate opportunities.

By engaging on industry-relevant posts, you'll start to build your personal brand, which will be noticed by prospects and peers.

And there it is, 3 simple 5-minute activities, just 15 minutes per day that done on a regular basis has the potential to generate some pretty awesome results.

Now you could spend 20 minutes a day, 30 minutes or more.

The key is to make sure you're **INVESTING** that time and not wasting it. Invest it in the right activities and you'll generate a far greater return. Smart salespeople don't waste time, they focus it on activities that generate the best possible results.

BONUS CHAPTER – The ABC's Of Social Selling

Glengarry Glen Ross featuring Alec Baldwin created the popular sales phrase:

"Always Be Closing"

His speech to motivate the team to stop waiting around for sales and instead to focus on getting them the buy has helped plenty of sales professionals over the years. This was actually a very effective approach in the old age where selling required more push.

To be fair, closing sales is still a big part of sales success.

Unless you close the sale there is no sale; everything else means nothing until the deal is done. However, the way we close and in fact, the way we sell has changed over the years.

Part of that change includes the introduction of social media into the sales process.

Social Selling is quite simply the effective use of social media the sales process. Sales professionals can use social media to find, connect and communicate with prospects and customers in the same way they might use the phone, email or face to face.

With people now spending a lot of time on social media every day, it has become a crucial platform to help salespeople reach more people and enhance the way they sell.

There are key fundamentals to achieving success with social selling, a lot of salespeople spend a lot of time on social without generating many, if any, results. It's the same as those sales professionals who don't know how to cold call effectively, making 100's of calls every day with no results at the end.

The key is to learn how to do it properly.

To help, here are the ABC's of Social Selling that focuses on those core fundamentals:

1) Always Be CONNECTING

The first ABC of Social Selling is to Always Be Connecting. Effective social selling comes from your ability to find and connect with potential prospects and customers. The more prospects and customers that you have in your network, the more opportunities you'll be able to generate in the short and long term.

My Top Tip: There are many great methods that you can search for prospects on LinkedIn, but when actually connecting with people, it's often worth making the effort to your LinkedIn connection request. Nothing to sales rich, just a simple and light. To bring this tip to life set yourself a goal to connect with X amount of new people every single day. It could be 5; it could be 10, whichever number works for you.

2) Always Be CREATING CONTENT

The 2nd ABC is to Always Be Creating Content. Successful social sellers create engaging and great personal content to share with their network of prospects and customers. Their content helps showcase their expertise, build trust and start the all-important sales conversations.

My Top Tip: Your content shouldn't be about your product but should be about YOU and your thoughts/knowledge/expertise. Create content such as posts, blogs, videos and images that offer value, insight, and knowledge which will then draw people to your profile and website where you can then leverage that to start conversations.

3) Always Be (starting) CONVERSATIONS

One of the most important fundamentals and ABC number 3 is Always Be (starting) Conversations. Social media is fun, likes and followers make us feel popular and important, but they certainly don't equate to pipeline and revenue until you turn them into REAL conversations that become meetings, pitches, and presentations.

My Top Tip: When you share great content, and you get likes and comments, use it to start a conversation via messenger. It might be a thank you or an opportunity to discuss the topic further. Those conversations can then potentially be worked into sales conversations if they are a qualified prospect.

4) Always Be CONSISTENT

The last ABC is to Always Be Consistent. Social Selling success comes from it on a daily basis. For example, if you only cold call someone once, and they don't answer, that's it. It's the same with if you do some social activity but then don't for a period of time, the results won't come. You need to build it into your sales process and it every day.

My Top Tip: Set time every single day to do social selling activities. It could be 15 - 30 minutes at the start of the day to connect with people, send messages and write a post.

You may then touch base at lunchtime to do the same, and again at the end of the day. Set it your calendar to ensure that time is focused on social.

And there they are, my ABC's of Social Selling! Simple, but very powerful. Use them regularly and consistently and you'll start to see results before you know it.

Every day you come into office always make sure you practice you're A, B, C's...

THE A,B,C OF SOCIAL SELLING

A - ALWAYS GIVE VALUE

B - BUILD YOUR BRAND

C - CONSISTENCY IS KEY

DANIEL DISNEY

Recommended Reading

I wanted to give you a few recommendations of other Social Selling and other Sales books that I would highly recommend:

Top Social Selling Books

COMBO Prospecting by Tony J Hughes

Social Selling Mastery by Jamie Shanks

Social Selling by Timothy Hughes

LinkedIn Unlocked by Melonie Dodaro

The LinkedIn Sales Playbook by Brynne Tillman

The Future of the Sales Profession by Graham Hawkins

Top Sales Books

The Extremely Successful Salesman's Club by Chris Murray

The No.1 Best Seller by Lee Bartlett

Sales EQ by Jeb Blount

The Only Sales Guide You'll Ever Need by Anthony Iannarino

The Sales Bible by Jeffrey Gitomer

GAP Selling by Keenan

To Sell Is Human by Daniel Pink

The Perfect Close by James Muir

The Sales Development Playbook by Trish Bertuzzi

High Profit Prospecting by Mark Hunter

The 10X Rule by Grant Cardone

Selling from The Heart by Larry Levine

Everybody Works in Sales by Niraj Kapur

Secrets of Successful Sales by Alison Edgar

Sales Success Stories by Scott Ingram

The 25 Sales Habits by Stephen Schiffman

Spin Selling by Neil Rackham

Advanced Selling Strategies by Brian Tracy

The Lost Art of Cold Calling by Matt Wanty

The Smart Selling Book by Mark Edwards

Seven Stories by Mike Adams

Rebirth of The Salesman by Cian Mcloughlin

Sales Mind by Helen Kensett

Selling with Ease by Chris Murray

Sales Glue by Matt Sykes

Key Person of Influence by Daniel Priestly

Eat Their Lunch by Anthony Iannarino

FREE eBook

"100 Amazing Social Selling Tips."

I really hope you've enjoyed this book and have taken a lot away from it! Hopefully, this has helped to bring LinkedIn messaging to life and given you somewhere to start with using it more effectively to start more conversations, create more sales pipeline and generate more clients.

If you did enjoy the book, I would be hugely grateful if you could leave an **Amazon review** for it.

If you do, I'd love to say thank you by giving you a copy of my eBook "100 Amazing Social Selling Tips" for free. All you need to do is leave an Amazon review and email me to show me that you've done it. I'll then send you a copy.
Thank you!

The Daily Sales

Founded and run by Daniel Disney, The Daily Sales mission is to help motivate, inspire, educate and entertain salespeople all over the world. Sharing a mixture of the best sales blogs, articles, podcasts, videos, webinars, quotes, tips and meme's, it's LinkedIn's most popular page and community for salespeople.

We share the best content for salespeople and sales leaders every single day.

Our page on LinkedIn has over **450,000 followers** and growing, we have pages on Facebook, Twitter and Instagram, and you can subscribe to our newsletter on

Check out and follow our social media pages and find more great content at:

www.thedailysales.net.

SOCIAL SELLING MASTERCLASS
ONLINE

One of the BEST online LinkedIn & Social Selling courses out there!

Daniel Disney's ONLINE LinkedIn/Social Selling Masterclass is absolutely PACKED with everything you need to know to start selling more with LinkedIn.

The course has over 10 hours of training included with over 60 tutorial videos, 35 guides and templates, 7 eBooks, several webinars and so much more. You get 12 months access and can learn as and when you have time.

SPECIAL OFFER

As a thank you for buying my book I would like to offer you **50% discount** on the price of my online course!

It's available for £499 but if you insert this voucher code it will drop the price down to just £249 for 12 months FULL access. Use voucher code **BOOKOFFER** to get your discount and start learning today! www.socialsellingtraining.net

Are you looking for a Keynote Speaker for your event?

Daniel Disney is one of the most popular and in-demand Sales/Social Selling/Motivational keynote speakers out there right now.

His talks are absolutely packed with passion, energy, inspiration and knowledge. He will keep the audience's attention from start to finish and leave them energised, motivated and full of new tips.

Daniel speaks at events and conferences across the world in front of audiences of all sizes. One thing is for sure, if Daniel is speaking at your event, your audience won't be disappointed. Daniel has spoken at large conferences, events, corporate all-hands meetings, even on a boat!

Some of Daniel's popular talks include:

- Why Social Selling Is the Future of Sales
- The Top Social Selling/LinkedIn Trends
- The Million-Pound LinkedIn Message
- Digital Selling for Modern Sellers
- Leading Your Sales Team to Social Success
- Building A Digital Selling Strategy
- Creating LinkedIn Content That Goes Viral
- Social Selling in Just 15 Minutes Per Day
- Custom keynotes also available

"Daniel's Keynote was one of the most attended of the show. I feel I have learned a lot from him regarding Social Selling and look at him as being at the forefront of the Social Selling Revolution."

To enquire about Daniel speaking at your event, please send event details to contact@thedailysales.net. For more information and Daniel's showreel, visit www.danieldisney.net.

SOCIAL SELLING MASTERCLASS

Are you looking for LinkedIn or Social Selling training for your sales team or business?

Daniel Disney is one of the leading LinkedIn experts out there, whilst there are many LinkedIn trainers out there, very few actually practice what they preach and have achieved results like Daniel has.

His sell-out 1-Day **Social Selling Masterclass** has been delivered to companies large and small around the world and covers everything you need to know to leverage LinkedIn to its full potential.

Each delegate after the 1-day training will then join an exclusive online group for post-training support, as well as having 12 months access to the full ONLINE LinkedIn/Social Selling masterclass, giving them all the tools, they need to start generating results.

The online resource hub comes complete with over 60 video tutorials, 35 guides & templates, webinars and a whole host of additional eBook, guides and Social Selling/LinkedIn resources.

You'll learn:

- How to build the ultimate lead generating LinkedIn profile
- How to find all of your prospects through LinkedIn's search filters
- How to build a personal brand that generates sales
- How to find great content to share
- How to create great content to share
- How to turn engagement into sales opportunities
- What tools are there to help
- How to deliver real results from social

And so, so much more

"Daniel's Social Selling Masterclass was an extremely useful learning exercise for our team. We thought the Masterclass was worth every penny and will certainly use him again."

To discuss getting Daniel in to train your business or team, please email contact@thedailysales.net.

What Daniel's Customers Say:

I cannot praise Daniel highly enough.

Daniel's Social Selling Masterclass was an extremely useful learning exercise for our team. He had extensive knowledge on possible techniques that could be applied to our business. And provided exceptionally detailed training and insight on social selling, which we were able to put into practice immediately.

Daniel's attitude and personality were exemplary. He displayed a good knowledge of the subject and built up a rapport with the attendees in no time. Daniel was a brilliant tutor, excellent quality of delivery, depth of knowledge and also communicated really well with all delegates. Pacing, delivery, passion for the subject and level of knowledge were/are excellent.

Our team thoroughly enjoyed this course and learned a great deal from the day spent at our HQ. We thought the Masterclass was worth every penny and will certainly use him again.

Thank you again Daniel and keep up the great work you're doing in this space.

Tim Johnson – CSO at Visualsoft

If Social selling is your game, then Daniel Disney is the name you need to know!! A fantastically engaging and insightful workshop, Daniel really knows how to help you get the most from it!

Every member of our team got something worthwhile from it and within days we have all been trying new techniques and venturing into the seeming scary world of Blogs and Vlogs(it's not as scary as it first seems!)

I cannot rate Daniels workshop highly enough and it is a must for anybody looking to improve their social media performance.

Gavin Dawson – Managing Director at CamAce Ltd

I would thoroughly recommend Daniel and his sessions on social selling, I recently attended one of his sessions and since then have a seen a huge improvement on my use of social media.

After a few tentative attempts at interesting and engaging posts I seemed to hit a note with people and had over 4000 views on a simple picture. I don't have anywhere near 4000 connections. My profile views jumped by over 700% and have had many connection requests.

Graham Cameron – Barclay Communications

I recently attended Daniel's "Social Selling Masterclass". Daniel has been there seen it done it! and his workshop was excellent, with his incredible experience and insights shared alongside dispelling some common myths about social media selling.

Daniel's enthusiasm, energy and experience were apparent during the day. I have implemented the learnings and results are coming in (on some prospects that I've been targeting for over 9 months!) .....

If you get the chance to attend this workshop you will not regret the investment. Daniel is one of the best Social media experts I've had the pleasure of meeting and working with.

Ian Beighton – Senior Vice President Business Development and Sales EMEA at Innovecs

I first met Daniel at the Sales Innovation Expo and had the pleasure of working with him as he was a Keynote Speaker for my show and his Keynote was one of the most attended of the show.

His dedication and diligence to his profession is a testament to the company he has built from scratch. I look at him as being at the forefront of the 'Social Selling Revolution'.

Gavin Harris – Director of B2B Marketing Expo

Special Thanks

I wanted to just say thank you to the people that have had a huge impact on my career and helped me get to where I am today. I am so grateful to everyone on this list and can't thank you enough for the help and support that you have given me.

My Mum & Sister – You've always pushed me to be the best I can, challenging me to work harder along the way. You taught me to understand the mind and understand people, skills that have been crucial in my career in sales.

Debbie (My First Sales Manager) – You saw something in me and supported me in my first real sales job. You were one of the best salespeople and sales leaders I ever had the fortune to work with.

Chris Murray – Your book, The Extremely Successful Salesman's Club is my all-time favourite sales book and it has been a true privilege to get to know you, work with you and call you my friend. You are a true sales legend.

Lee Bartlett – Meeting you 3 years ago was the most amazing experience. Your book The No.1 Best Seller is one of my top 3 all-time sales books, and you've been a huge support throughout my sales journey.

Niraj Kapur – You've been one of the biggest supporters in me writing this book and your coaching has been a huge help.

Louise – You hired me to deliver my first-ever LinkedIn/Social Selling workshop and supported me with lots of work during my first year self-employed. You were one of my biggest supporters; thank you!

Gavin Ingham – You truly are one of the most motivational people in the world and you've been an amazing mentor and friend to me. I remember spending hours talking before I launched my business, you helped me find the confidence to do it and have helped me grow it.

Dad – You never worked in sales, but you would have been great. You taught me to work harder than anyone else, to never boast but instead let my results do the talking. You also taught me to draw, and whilst I'm nowhere near the artist that you are, I hope my doodles help others.

Tony Goodchild – We met just as I had started all of this, and you blew me away with your sales platform, Sales Pitch Pro. You're such an amazing and genuine person and I can't wait to see Sales Pitch Pro become a big player in sales.

Darryl Praill – You are a true legend, and your support has been a huge part of my journey. Our debates have been brilliant, and I've loved working with you and the team at VanillaSoft. It's no surprise it's the best Sales Engagement platform out there.

Thank you to everyone who has worked with me, hired me and supported me over the years! Thank you to everyone who booked me to speak, hired me to train their team or who become partner with The Daily Sales.

Your support is massively appreciated, and I look forward to hopefully working together for years to come.

Thank You!

One final thank you ...to YOU the reader!

Thank you again for buying this book. It always makes me so happy to meet business owners, salespeople, sales leaders, entrepreneurs etc. who want to use LinkedIn and social selling.

I really do hope you enjoyed this book and took as much away from it as possible.

You can find out more about me, my speaking and training along with blogs and other social selling content at **www.danieldisney.net**.

Please do follow me on LinkedIn & Twitter:

LinkedIn: https://uk.linkedin.com/in/danieldisney

Twitter: @thedandisney

If you have any questions at all, please feel free to email me at contact@thedailysales.net.

Happy Social Selling!

Daniel Disney

Printed in Great Britain
by Amazon